HERMÈS,
BEAUTY IS A GESTURE

ROUGE HERMÈS, SHADE 64 - ROUGE CASAQUE

PARACHUTE

For life at home.

parachutehome.com

53 CHAIR & SOFA 1953

TF Design
Modern Designs in Resin

tf.design

tf

KINFOLK

MAGAZINE	**EDITOR-IN-CHIEF**	John Clifford Burns
	EDITOR	Harriet Fitch Little
	ART DIRECTOR	Christian Møller Andersen
	DESIGN DIRECTOR	Alex Hunting
	COPY EDITOR	Rachel Holzman
STUDIO	**ADVERTISING, SALES & DISTRIBUTION DIRECTOR**	Edward Mannering
	STUDIO & PROJECT MANAGER	Susanne Buch Petersen
	DESIGNER & ART DIRECTOR	Staffan Sundström
	DIGITAL MANAGER	Cecilie Jegsen
	CO-FOUNDER	Nathan Williams

STYLING, SET DESIGN, HAIR & MAKEUP

Salem Charabi, Evan Feng, Andreas Frienholt, Helena Henrion, Marie Labarre, Katy Lassen, Martin Persson, Rasmus Stroyberg, Camille-Joséphine Teisseire, Whitney Whitaker, Daniel Zhang

WORDS

Alex Anderson, Katie Calautti, James Clasper, Stephanie d'Arc Taylor, Michelle Dean, Cody Delistraty, Daphnée Denis, Tom Faber, Bella Gladman, Harry Harris, Tim Hornyak, Robert Ito, Ana Kinsella, Hugo Macdonald, Stevie Mackenzie-Smith, Kyla Marshell, Megan Nolan, Debika Ray, Asher Ross, Tristan Rutherford, Laura Rysman, Caspar Salmon, Ben Shattuck, Pip Usher, Annick Weber

ARTWORK & PHOTOGRAPHY

Jasper Abels, Gustav Almestål, Luc Braquet, Steven Brooke, Alexis Christodoulou, Justin Chung, Lea Colie Wight, Cristina Coral, Pelle Crépin, Katrien De Blauwer, Ben Duggan, Hans Feurer, Franco Fontana, Paul Godard, Zahra Holm, Mary Kang, Sebastian Kim, Paloma Lanna, Tana Latorre, Geraint Lewis, Alexander Liberman, Matthieu Litt, Jesse Marble, Christian Møller Andersen, Ilaria Orsini, Jonathan Daniel Pryce, Paul Rousteau, Heather Sten, Armin Tehrani, Zoltan Tombor, Jumbo Tsui, Annemarieke van Drimmelen, Marieke Verdenius, Stephen Voss, Andre D. Wagner

CROSSWORD	Anna Gundlach
PUBLICATION DESIGN	Alex Hunting Studio
COVER PHOTOGRAPH	Jumbo Tsui

Kinfolk (ISSN 2596-6154) is published quarterly by Ouur ApS, Amagertorv 14, 1, 1160 Copenhagen, Denmark. Printed by Park Communications Ltd in London, United Kingdom. Color reproduction by Park Communications Ltd in London, United Kingdom. All rights reserved. No part of this publication may be reproduced, distributed or transmitted in any form or by any means, including photocopying or other electronic or mechanical methods, without prior written permission of the editor in chief, except in the case of brief quotations embodied in critical reviews and certain other noncommercial uses permitted by copyright law. The US annual subscription price is $87 USD. Airfreight and mailing in the USA by WN Shipping USA, 156-15, 146th Avenue, 2nd Floor, Jamaica, NY 11434, USA. Application to mail at periodicals postage prices is pending at Jamaica NY 11431. US Postmaster: Send address changes to Kinfolk, WN Shipping USA, 156-15, 146th Avenue, 2nd Floor, Jamaica, NY 11434, USA. Subscription records are maintained at Ouur ApS, Amagertorv 14, 1, 1160 Copenhagen, Denmark. The views expressed in Kinfolk magazine are those of the respective contributors and are not necessarily shared by the company or its staff. SUBSCRIBE — Kinfolk is published four times a year. To subscribe, visit www.kinfolk.com/subscribe or email us at info@kinfolk.com. CONTACT US — If you have questions or comments, please write to us at info@kinfolk.com. For advertising and partnership inquiries, get in touch at advertising@kinfolk.com.

PORTUGUESE
KNOWLEDGE
Flannel
IN A
NEW WORLD

Starters

18   Wild Thoughts

20   Such Good News

21   Word: Hot Mess

24   Casa Scatturin

26   Reformed Characters

27   No More Mr. Average

28   Mood Bores

30   Fake Goods

31   Consider the Hot Tub

32   Wasted Journey

34   In Season: Arid Art

36   Joekenneth Museau

42   Mona Chalabi

18 – 48

Features

50   Haatepah Clearbear

60   Miyoko Yasumoto

70   Material Girl

78   Vizcaya Gardens

84   At Home With: Nanushka

90   Downsizing

98   Short Histories of Nearly Everything

102   Helen Frankenthaler

50 – 112

"There's a lot of beauty in the bizarre as it reveals the singularity of the maker."
MIYOKO YASUMOTO – P. 67

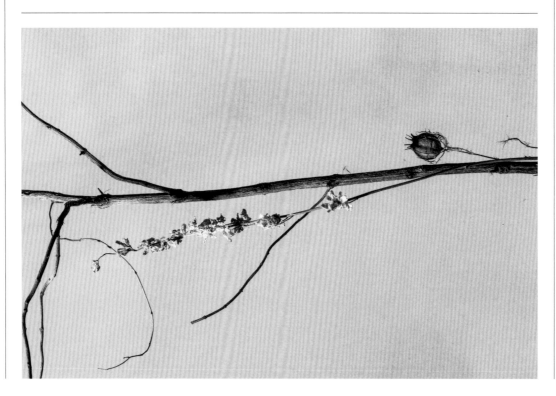

Photograph: Luc Braquet

Nature

114	Rendered Impossible
120	Ron Finley
128	The Click Farm
136	Fresh Press
144	Jane Goodall
152	The Force of Nature
156	Rock Steady
166	Five Tips

Directory

178	Peer Review
179	Object Matters
180	Cult Rooms
182	Bad Idea
183	Last Night
184	Anne Tyler
186	Crossword
187	Correction
189	Stockists
191	Credits
192	My Favorite Thing

114 – 176

178 – 192

"Look to nature, and you will soon find out where you are."
HARRY HARRIS – P. 172

Artwork: Alexis Christodoulou

String® Pocket metal Taupe with hooks.

Way back when we chose nature as the theme of our fall issue, we thought it would make for a summer well spent, with *Kinfolk* contributors fanning out to remote locations from which to explore the great outdoors. The restrictions imposed by a near-worldwide lockdown made that initial vision for this issue impossible.

But nature always finds a way. For our themed section, we were led by the creativity and ingenuity of our contributors. During the travel ban, Alexis Christodoulou, a self-taught 3D artist and designer based in Cape Town, conceived his series *Rendered Impossible* on page 114 as an opportunity to visit fantasy landscapes that exist nowhere beyond the pages of this magazine. Confined to their home in the south of France, photographer Paul Rousteau and set designer Marie Labarre picked and pressed flowers from their garden, using an ingenious scanning technique to create kaleidoscopic floral landscapes for the series *Fresh Press* on page 136. *Rock Steady*, the fashion editorial that covers this issue, took place among the ancient rock formations of southwestern China, where life had more or less returned to normal as the rest of the world stood still.

As we paced the corners of our makeshift home offices, we saw the importance of nature with new clarity. Specifically, we realized that small pockets of greenery deserve to be celebrated as much as sweeping vistas. Few are better placed to demonstrate this than Ron Finley, the urban gardener once issued with an arrest warrant for planting his LA sidewalk with vegetables and banana trees. The outcry was such that the decision was reversed and Finley has since become a proud community activist, encouraging people to grow on every scrap of land available. "Gardening is the most therapeutic and defiant act you can do, especially in the inner city," he says on page 120. Finley's story is an exclusive preview from our forthcoming book, *The Kinfolk Garden*. Publishing on October 27, it digs deeper into how to live with nature.

Elsewhere, we meet Haatepah Clearbear, the young model advocating for the future of Native Americans—and the planet; we take a crash course in floristry with Parisian floral artist Miyoko Yasumoto; and we crunch some numbers with data journalist Mona Chalabi. While stuck indoors, our minds have wandered to some strange places. In this issue our writers answer questions including: Why are popular science books suddenly so, well, popular? What could you teach a caveman? And why do some animals have more followers than humans on Instagram?

JOHN CLIFFORD BURNS & HARRIET FITCH LITTLE

1.

18 — 48

Starters

18
Wild Thoughts

21
Word: Hot Mess

28
Mood Bores

30
Fake Goods

31
Consider the Hot Tub

36
Joekenneth Museau

41
Hobbyhorses

42
Mona Chalabi

Wild Thoughts

On the nature of nature writing.

Photograph: Jesse Marble

Scottish poet Kathleen Jamie deftly skewered the stereotypical nature writer in a 2008 article for the *London Review of Books*: "What's that coming over the hill? A white, middle-class Englishman! A Lone Enraptured Male! From Cambridge! Here to boldly go, 'discovering'."

"I went to the woods because I wished to live deliberately… and not, when I came to die, discover that I had not lived," Henry David Thoreau famously wrote in *Walden*, his account of two years spent in a cabin on the shores of Walden Pond in Massachusetts. His exploration of man's relationship to the natural world, and his quest for an existence stripped of artifice, is widely considered to be one of the foundational pieces of nature writing—a beloved literary genre where science and introspection meet. Yet his musings also elicit eye rolls. Thoreau barely removed himself from the society he so despised, one argument goes, since he was able to regularly return to his family home to drop off his dirty laundry. One infamous *New Yorker* essay deemed him "pinched and selfish," and his work "the original cabin porn."

While it's unclear how many 19th-century writers washed their own clothes, there's plenty of evidence that Thoreau wasn't, in fact, a misanthropist, or a hypocrite: *Walden* isn't misleading as to the degree of isolation he lived in. Yet it is undeniable that issues of privilege permeate the conversation around nature writing, which Thoreau symbolizes, for better or for worse. Only certain groups of people have historically been able to venture out, unafraid. The concept of environmental writing, a form of literature that separates nature from the people living in it, tends to romanticize its subject matter in a way that can appear unrealistic. Still today, the canon of nature writers is predominantly composed of white men, since the genre, which originated in the United Kingdom, blossomed during the European colonization of America.

"There's this idea, which doesn't apply to all American nature writing, that a privileged white man goes into an empty wild space, only empty of course because the native people who used to live there have been killed off or removed," says Karla Armbruster, an English professor at Webster University. She points out however, that Thoreau's critics seem to confuse him with John Muir—known as "the father of the national park system"—who seemed to care more for non-human life than for the Native Americans and African Americans he demeaned in his writings.

At the heart of the problem lies the issue of representation, argues Carolyn Finney, a scholar-in-residence at the Franklin Environmental Center at Middlebury College. Non-white writers have produced works about nature for centuries, and yet their contribution to the genre has been vastly ignored. "It's about who gets to claim: 'I belong here'—which is an ongoing fight in a country made up of immigrants, the ancestors of enslaved Africans, and indigenous people," Finney says. "Muir's perspective about nature isn't incorrect. It's just incomplete."

Environmental literature spans beyond the names—and views—of its most celebrated authors. It can be found in the observations of a city dweller looking out the window, as well as in the recollections of epic wilderness adventures. Much like its subject matter, the beauty of nature writing is that it can expand across boundaries. Let it grow free.
Words by Daphnée Denis

Such Good News

On the success of others.

"Some personal news." It's a phrase that most users of social media will be familiar with as a precursor to a positive announcement about someone's work or life—anything from a promotion to a pregnancy. The use of the phrase on Twitter has rapidly increased over the past decade, and is now even a meme. "Some exciting personal news: I have had enough," one tweet announces, capturing all of our feelings on the subject.

We encounter such declarations from people we barely know more frequently in the digital age. It's no coincidence that the word "humblebrag" was coined around the same time as Facebook and Twitter took over our lives. The purpose of posting personal revelations on social media, it seems, is mostly to fulfill a craving for praise and congratulations; if the motive was simply to spread joy, we'd only tell our nearest and dearest.

A study by psychologist Cara Palmer and her colleagues, published in 2016 in the *Journal of Individual Differences*, drew a distinction between capitalizing on good news (sharing with people close to you), bragging (sharing with those who may become jealous or upset) and mass-sharing (sharing with many people at once using communication technology), and found that men are more likely than women to be braggers, and that braggers are less agreeable, conscientious and empathic, i.e. more narcissistic than average.

Jutta Tobias Mortlock, a senior lecturer in the department of psychology at London's City University, has a different take. She believes there's something inherently well-meaning about sharing good news. "It's normally a prosocial act, an effort to lift the mood," she points out. In today's context, she says, "Maybe people intuitively think we need a bit more good news than normal, because the general mood is more somber."

In an environment like social media—specifically designed for public sharing, brand-building and for keeping tabs on others—irritation at the announcement of good news arguably misses the point. Nonetheless, it can grate—eliciting a kind of reverse schadenfreude, a mix of jealousy, resentment and annoyance. Mortlock speculates that our irritation at declarations of good news online is partly related to perceptions of falsity—we know we're seeing an airbrushed version of the truth.

It's less obvious why we might find it hard to hear good news from those close to us. Often, of course, it's simply envy; at a time when many lives are difficult, it's no surprise that good news can be painful to hear. And in societies driven by consumption and acquisition, we're taught that a successful life is measured by landmark achievements. The inevitable consequence is that we assess ourselves against the life events of others; so hearing good news (especially news that mirrors goals we're striving for ourselves) can highlight our own failures—at least on the terms set by the wider world. "If you're not in a good place, it's hard to see others being happy," says Mortlock.

It's important, then, when sharing good news to be mindful of others' suffering. "Sharing extreme happiness in a boastful or callous way can feel inappropriate, especially at a time when many people are living difficult lives," she says. "Respect and compassion doesn't cost anything."
Words by Debika Ray

Photograph: Jonathan Daniel Pryce

WOMEN LOOKING AT WOMEN

by Harriet Fitch Little

When we look at a female nude, whose eyes are we seeing her through? For most of art history, naked women have been painted by male artists. "Men look at women. Women watch themselves being looked at," wrote John Berger—the British art critic who revolutionized the contemporary understanding of authorship in art with his 1972 BBC series, *Ways of Seeing.* Not any more. Admire a female nude in a gallery today, and it's far more likely to be of the artist herself than of an anonymous model. Controlling how one's own body gets portrayed is an expression of power—like in these self-portraits by Paloma Lanna, reinterpreted as cut-outs by her frequent collaborator Tana Latorre.

Word: Hot Mess

From humble grub to humblebrag.

Etymology: First coined to describe a hot meal, the term's sloppy connotations quickly morphed from food-related to figurative when it came to reference a chaotic yet appealing individual.

Meaning: Stand-up comedian Amy Schumer has amassed a multimillion-dollar fortune through being a hot mess. Her ribald humor—which riffs on binge-drinking, body parts and bad sex—has established this identity as her shtick, so much so that billboards advertising her show, *Inside Amy Schumer,* were branded with the phrase.

Ask a soldier in the late 19th century to describe a hot mess, however, and he'd launch into details of the canteen meal he'd just scoffed. A literal descriptor of a warm, mushy meal prepared in bulk, the word's origins can be traced to the Latin root, "missus," meaning a portion of food. The term jumped into American lingo to describe slapdash, troublesome scenarios. A 1912 biography describes former President Andrew Jackson as "pretty apt to make a nice hot mess." From there, it was a short jump from situational label to personal.

A decade ago, "hot mess" entered the mainstream with *Project Runway* contestant Christian Siriano's finger-clicking usage. Since then, it has been applied both as an insult—"What a hot mess," you might say of someone whose dysfunction leads them from one disaster to another—and as a badge of honor. In recent years, enough high-profile women have appropriated the phrase for journalist Eileen G'Sell to label this form of self-identification as a "hot mess humblebrag."

It seems curious to boast of one's failings. Yet on closer examination, it's the type of self-deprecation that works only when someone's formidable achievements suggest otherwise. If you're wildly successful, claims of chaotic behavior can lend a winsome air of relatability. But for the rest of us, there's nothing hot about it—it's simply a big, stinking mess.

Words by Pip Usher

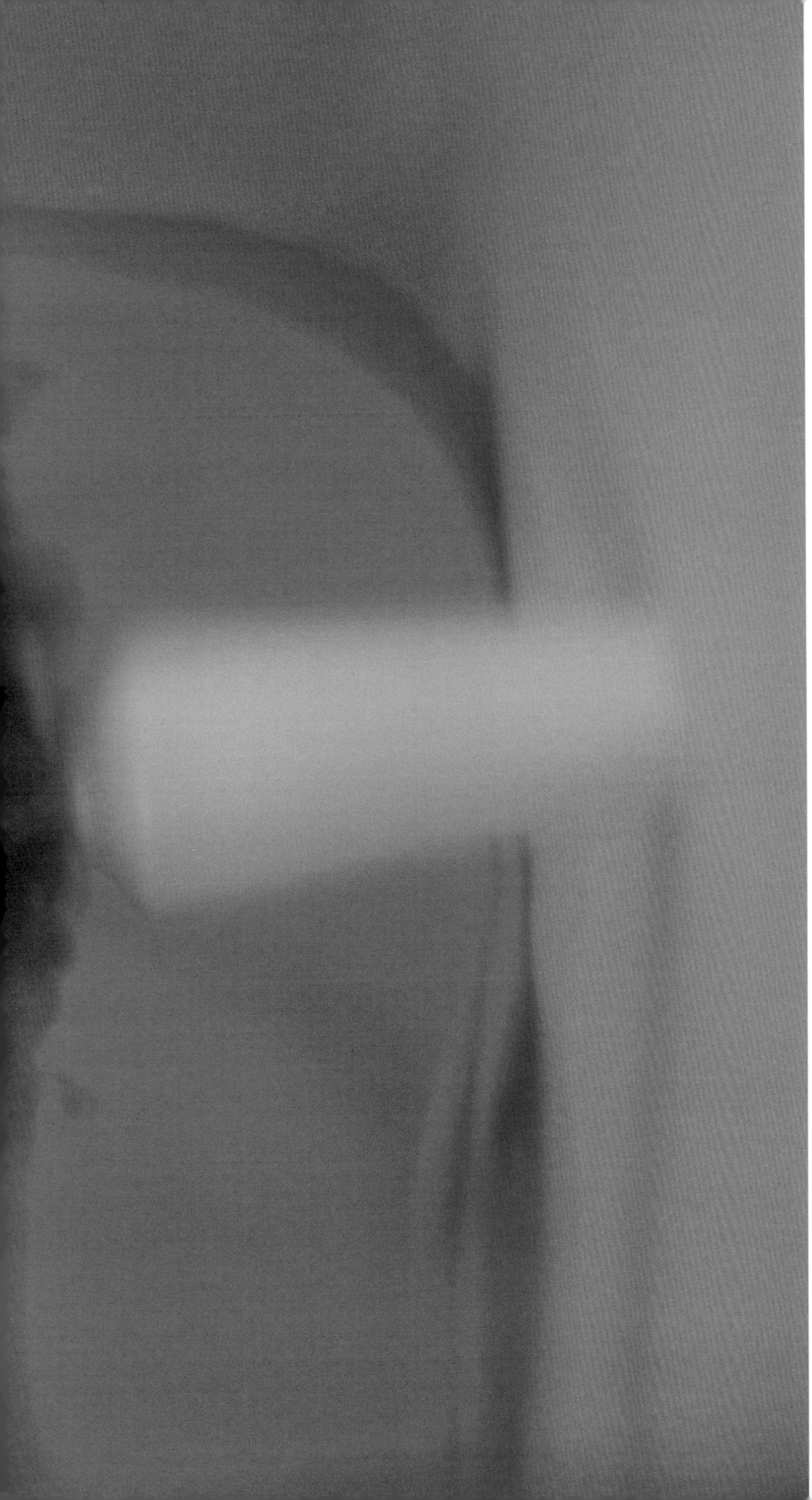

POLLEN COUNTS

by Tom Faber

In 1997, a woman in Christchurch, New Zealand, was raped in an alleyway. She described the assailant to the police and a man was arrested, but he denied having committed the crime and there was no DNA evidence. The case looked hopeless until an unexpected witness emerged—a flowering wormwood shrub that had been damaged in the struggle. Native to the Mediterranean, it's an uncommon plant in New Zealand; and when a forensic lab examined the suspect's jeans, they found a pollen match with 99.9% accuracy. This evidence was used at trial to sentence the man to eight years in prison.

The field of forensic botany may be less popular than fingerprint or ballistic analysis, but it's just as useful. There are around 400,000 plant species on earth, each with a unique pollen type which can be used to tie people to a place and time with remarkable accuracy.

Forensic botany can also help uncover patterns of movement around crimes. In New Jersey in the 1930s, an early expert identified the wood in a ladder found at the scene of the Lindbergh baby kidnapping and traced it to a shop near the suspect's house. After the Bosnian war, forensic botanists traced bodies from mass graves to their original burial sites. And a headless, limbless torso floating in the River Thames in London was linked to Nigeria by a seed found in the stomach. Yet there are vanishingly few forensic botanists: Only one is employed full-time in the United States. The discipline requires extensive knowledge and its relevance is often underestimated by police. So it may be some time before *CSI: Botanical Strike Force* hits our screens. *Photograph by Paul Rousteau*

Casa Scatturin

Law and domestic order in Carlo Scarpa's Venice.

In 1963, renovation works began on the top floor of a 17th-century Venetian palazzo that would see it transformed into a sprawling residential and office space for a lawyer named Luigi Scatturin. The result—a modernist masterpiece whose many attractive attributes include pearwood walls, a set of narrow, two-tone stairs that stack upward like building blocks, and bespoke furniture—took three years to complete. It was only following Scatturin's death more than 50 years later, when Casa Scatturin was placed on the market, that its spectacular interior could be (briefly) appreciated by those beyond its owner and his immediate circle.

Since then, the property has been heralded as an iconic piece in the portfolio of its creator, Carlo Scarpa. A Venetian architect who maintained a fierce loyalty to the artisanal traditions of his region, Scarpa built a reputation on his ability to fuse such ancient craft with wildly contemporary design. [1] Despite his acclaim, Scarpa never officially qualified as an architect, refusing to take the government exams after his studies at Venice's Academy of Fine Arts. [2] This contrarian decision would later prove problematic: When Scarpa was charged with practicing architecture without a license, it was Scatturin who successfully represented him in court. Grateful, Scarpa decided to redesign Scatturin's home.

For many of his devotees, Scarpa has long been overlooked in the lineup of modernist greats. Scatturin, though, was wise to his friend's talents all along: In 1990, he registered the apartment as "vincolo," granting it the same heritage status as St. Mark's Basilica, Venice's most famous church.
Words by Pip Usher

NOTES

1. Scarpa's structures make up the majority of Venice's modernist legacy. However, several of his peers worked on projects for the city that never got built, including Le Corbusier (a hospital) and Isamu Noguchi (a park). Frank Lloyd Wright's 1953 design for a waterfront residence was rejected as aesthetically inappropriate.

2. Scarpa's refusal to officially qualify as an architect changed the course of his career. He became best known for his interiors, and for updating pre-existing buildings. Among his most celebrated projects is the renovation of the 14th-century Castelvecchio Museum in Verona.

THE SPOTLIGHT EFFECT

by Pip Usher

Should a new haircut go awry, it's normal to find yourself wanting to hide from side-eyes and sniggering. If it goes well, you may feel you leave the salon basking in the glow of strangers' approving glances. But according to social psychologists, both scenarios exist mostly in your head. The "spotlight effect" refers to the mistaken belief that other people notice our actions and appearances as much as we do. Because our engagement with the world is shaped by a singular set of biases, we overestimate the weight of our experiences and conclude that others have done the same. It's an egocentric and unreliable barometer. In truth, other people are too busy making the same erroneous assumption about us.

Reformed Characters

Should adaptations read between the lines?

In *Casino Royale*, James Bond orders a vodka martini, and is asked, "shaken or stirred?" "Do I look like I give a damn?" he spits back tersely—a clever, if facile, way of signaling that the character had moved on since his early days of fussy tux-wearing and silly gadgetry. Daniel Craig's 007, we gathered, was to be more of a bruised everyman than the perma-coiffed spy played by his predecessor, Pierce Brosnan. This delighted fans of the franchise, but raised questions about how far from their roots a character could stray.

This past winter, Greta Gerwig tested the limits of this idea with a free-flowing adaptation of *Little Women*, which essentially rewrote the relationship between Jo and Laurie, and which gave us a wholly new Amy, as played by Florence Pugh. Amy had always been a problematic character in Louisa May Alcott's coming-of-age novel, particularly for on-screen adaptations. How to leaven her acts of cruelty—her burning of Jo's manuscript, and her relationship with Laurie that seems to be entered into out of spite toward her sister? Gerwig and Pugh turn Amy inside out, giving us a character who exists somewhere outside the 19th century's conventions of goodness and wickedness; here is a fleshed out woman who resists categorization, whose very ambiguity makes her compelling. In that transformation, though, Gerwig may have betrayed some of the book's spirit; and perhaps rendered Jo, her apparent main character, *less* compelling.

In contemporary readings of Shakespeare and other classical plays it is de rigueur to impose a new spin on certain characters. *The Taming of the Shrew*'s Katherine may be rendered less caustic; Shylock can be redeemed. Andrew Scott recently treated Londoners to a thoroughly modern, relatable Hamlet, far from the mania of many other productions. These acts of revisionism can give urgency and vitality to characters—yet arguably they take us far from their roots, sometimes into the realms of invention altogether. At such times, creators test the limits of adaptability, which come when characters become unrecognizable. James Bond was in fact a very specific, detailed creation—a nihilist at a time of nuclear threat; a preening misogynist; a disdainful and racist product of the British empire. When we shear him of those labels, are we also chipping away at history?

Words by Caspar Salmon

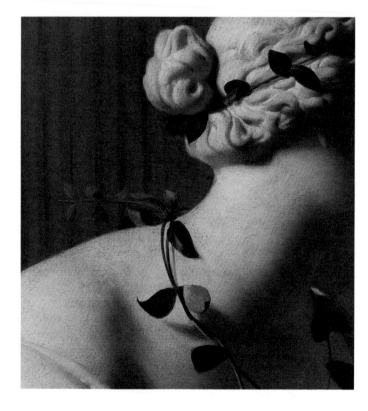

Previous page: Photograph: Ilaria Orsini. Left Photograph: Jasper Abels. Right Photograph: *Trompe l'Oeil with a Bust of Venus*, Caesar van Everdingen, 1665. Courtesy of Mauritshuis, The Hague.

Photograph: *Alternative Perspective Trio*, Cristina Coral, 2017.

No More Mr. Average

The case for grand delusions.

In 1994, West Ham United were playing against Oxford United, when one of their players got injured. Their manager, Harry Redknapp, having used all his substitutes, turned to a West Ham fan in the crowd named Steve Davies, who'd spent most of the first half criticizing striker Lee Chapman. "Do you play as good as you talk?" Redknapp asked. "I'm better than that Chapman," Davies replied, and so on to the pitch he went.

Davies was likely indulging in what's known as the "superiority illusion," a trait whereby we believe we're above average at whatever we happen to set our mind to. Psychologist David Dunning has studied the effect for years, and argues that the majority of people succumb to the illusion in some form. The statistics bear it out: 65% of Americans believe they're smarter than most and 90% percent of drivers think they're better than average. When it comes to positive traits, people tend to score themselves highly.

There's evidence to suggest that the superiority illusion is a shield for our mental health. One of the traits associated with depression is a high connectivity between the frontal cortex of the brain, responsible for our sense of self, and the striatum, responsible for reward processing, which causes what's known as "depressive realism." For the majority of us, having a lower connectivity between those two areas gives us a better view of ourselves. And according to the Dunning-Kruger effect—named for David Dunning and his fellow psychologist Justin Kruger—the more incompetent you are at something, the more likely you are to overestimate your ability at it.

Surprisingly, that wasn't the case for Steve Davies. In fact, after he came on in that game, the West Ham fan scored. Recounting the story two decades on, Redknapp conceded that on that day Davies was, true to his word, "better than Chapman." Amazing what a little self-belief can do for you. *Words by Harry Harris*

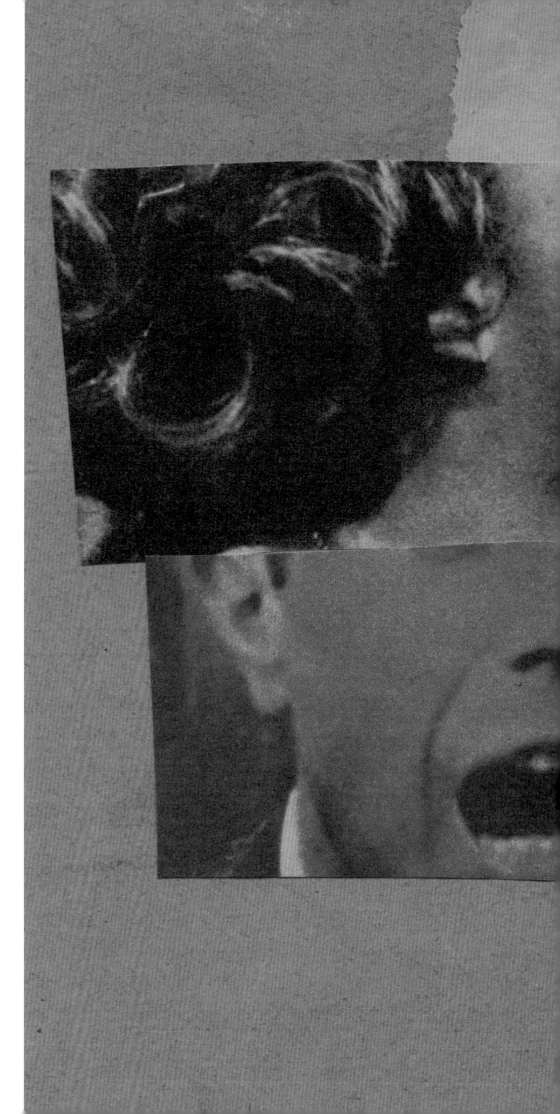

GALLERY VIEW

by Pip Usher

A gallery wall adds a snapshot of your personality to a home interior. Quirky artworks, flea market finds and mementos from exotic travels; a jumbled assortment of framed prints, often hung like a jigsaw puzzle, serves as a declaration of interests and tastes. But in recent years, gallery walls have had some of their rough edges rounded off. As these stylized interiors have become increasingly popular, DIY kits have surfaced to supply a pre-selected curation of framed prints that look eerily similar to the color-coordinated interiors of Instagram, where they may first have been viewed.

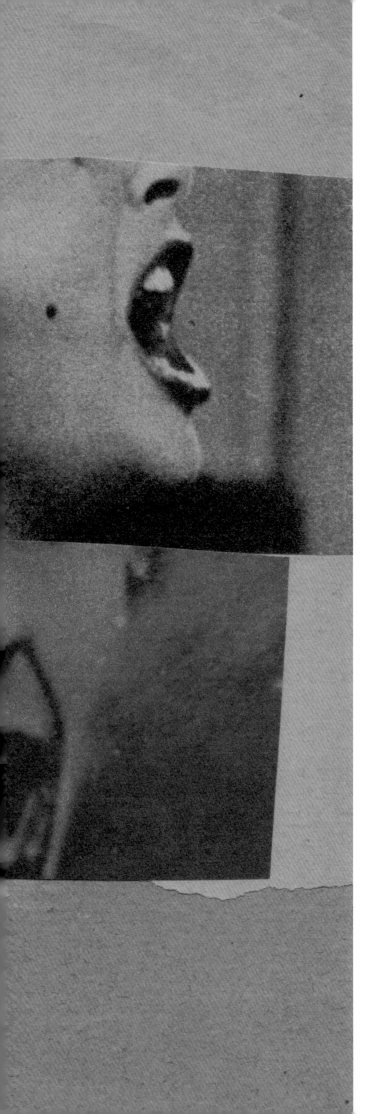

Mood Bores

On the aesthetics of inspiration.

On social media, everyone is an artist. Or at least it can seem that way as we scroll through an endless stream of charming snapshots of writing desks, sketchbooks and moodboards. The artistic process, regardless of what it might or might not produce, is a lifestyle statement. You might be wondering where the fruit of all this beautifully documented labor is. No need: The focus here is on the process itself.

There has always been something alluring about the mystery of creativity. That's understandable; a great work of art *is* mystifying, and it's natural to be curious about the steps taken to create it. But while many of us may dream of making art, what platforms like Instagram have done is shift the focus from the art itself to the creative process, as a product to be marketed and profited from.

Even the rough work of scrapbooks and collages is now treated as a commodity. *The New York Times* reported earlier this year that canny influencers are selling ready-made collage kits for bedroom walls—themed bundles of images in coordinating tones. A search on Etsy provides thousands of results for products to help you build a vision board of your own. Some promise to help customers "manifest good success," or accomplish various dreams and goals. The step-by-step method of looking for inspiration and gathering it together, using the creative energy of one's own internal furnace, can now be outsourced to a stranger online, and the results have a curiously streamlined appearance.

There's a debate to be had about the value of vision boards—a 2011 study published in the *Journal of Experimental Social Psychology* suggested that time spent creating vision boards might be better spent realizing your vision—but their popularity has created a billion-dollar industry. In 2019, the online scrapbook platform Pinterest was valued at over $10 billion when it began trading on the New York Stock Exchange. The internet provides the would-be creator with the tools she needs to get started; for advertisers, this represents a gold mine of potential revenue.

Of course, there are benefits for the creator, too. Through the prism of late capitalism, the very term "creative" takes on new meaning. In his 2002 book, *The Rise of the Creative Class*, economist and social scientist Richard Florida pinpointed the growth of a new subset of worker and, in doing so, identified creativity as an economic force. This doesn't require writing novels or painting masterpieces: The worker who describes herself as creative on her CV is more likely to be referring to her flexibility and adaptability in the workplace. Creativity becomes a marketable skill of its own.

In reality, the process of making art is a messy thing, and one that is not easily packaged and sold. Artists and writers will tell you that writing a novel or painting a masterpiece is a time-intensive piece of labor, one that involves personal sacrifice and that can come at the expense of a balanced life. Like almost everything, the truth of it is rarely as photogenic as the images on social media might have you believe.
Words by Ana Kinsella

Left Photograph: Zahra Holm. Right Artwork: Katrien De Blauwer

Fake Goods

On the alluring pros of cons.

What is it about certain scammers that beguiles so? There are plenty of people who commit fraud, tell lies and manipulate others for their own gain, but not all capture the public imagination. Those who do become something strange in our collective consciousness: not heroes, not to be emulated, but not villains either. They occupy a space somewhere between "I can't believe someone did that" and "Could I do that?"

The likes of Anna Delvey—the imprisoned Russian faux-socialite who scammed New York elites and hotels to the tune of $275,000—are capable of charming us partly because their victims are not ordinary people. Nobody finds the fraudster conning grandmothers out of pensions alluring or seductive. But we can allow ourselves to indulge in salacious enjoyment of Delvey's crimes because those who were swindled had so very much to lose in the first place. Elizabeth Holmes, the disgraced CEO of medical technology company Theranos, is set to stand trial in August for committing massive fraud by fabricating claims about her company's ability to test blood droplets for disease, raising $9 billion for it in the process. Theranos was a company that produced, in the end, nothing at all. But it was sustained by the sheer force of Holmes' persona. She consciously curated the airs and aesthetics of a dynamic, singular CEO genius, and used this adopted personality to elicit vast sums from those all too eager to buy into it.

Most interesting of all are the repeat scammers like Frank Abagnale and Ferdinand Demara, both of whom successfully assumed many false identities and occupations—Abagnale in the 1960s and Demara in the 1940s. The former was immortalized in film by Leonardo DiCaprio, the latter by Tony Curtis. Both were brilliant at fraud, yes, but they tried their hands at many other things too. They were self-taught, amazingly intelligent pretenders, who could have legitimately become the pilots or doctors they characterized if they had chosen to.

But they didn't—they chose to be imposters, to not just "be somebody" but to be many somebodies, whoever they felt like being. Self-invention is the American dream, after all. The best scammers simply take this cherished ideal to the next level. They allow us the brief, dazzling possibility of identity being as easily shrugged off and on as a coat. They create a reality in which to simply say you are a thing is to be it—where language and gesture overtake material circumstances.
Words by Megan Nolan

In Miranda July's new film, *Kajillionaire*, a family of small-time con artists spends a rare windfall on buying a hot tub. The pool looks comically out of place installed in the office building where they're squatting, and becomes a symbol of how far their aspirations are from their reality.

Photograph: Hans Feurer / Trunk Archive

Consider the Hot Tub

Cleaning up the history of steamy soaks.

People have most likely been submerging themselves in hot water since, well, before they were people; just look at those adorably furry Japanese macaques chilling out in snowy mountain *onsen*. We might have evolved past all that body hair, but soaking in hot water still feels good.

Natural mineral hot springs burbling out of volcanic mountains are one thing, but stand-alone Jacuzzi tubs are something else entirely. Given their popular reputation as a site of swinging '60s, quaalude-fueled romps, perhaps no one will be surprised to learn that the modern hot tub was invented in California. But the story behind that invention is as wholesome as apple pie. After immigrating to the US in the early 20th century from rural northwest Italy, Candido Jacuzzi settled with his parents and 12 siblings in Berkeley, California. Like most immigrants, they were entrepreneurial. Over 40 years, Jacuzzi Brothers Inc. registered more than 50 patents for industrial machinery,

for everything from pumps to aerospace propellers. When we think of 20th-century hot tubs, we envision a silk-robed Hugh Hefner type with a cocktail shaker, or maybe Santa Cruz nudists selling psychedelics out of their garage. When Candido Jacuzzi thought of 19th-century hot tubs, on the other hand, he saw doctors prescribing healing waters as a last-ditch therapy for a panoply of illnesses. Jacuzzi invented the eponymous tub when his 18-month-old son was diagnosed with rheumatoid arthritis. The first Jacuzzi was an attempt to relieve a child's pain, it wasn't meant to inspire couples to make a generation of new ones. So next time you hear the tinkle of Chardonnay glasses accompanied by telltale giggling coming from over the hedge, stifle your sniff. Your neighbors are probably far more relaxed than you are. And, who knows—maybe they would welcome some company.

Words by Stephanie d'Arc Taylor

Wasted Journey

What could you teach a caveman?

If you could send one piece of knowledge back to the Stone Age, what would it be? Assuming you're making this decision for the good of humankind rather than scheming to make yourself rich, your answer will likely depend on your definition of human progress.

You've got options. You can right a historic wrong. Introduce life-saving technology centuries early. Expedite a social revolution of your choice. You should try to offer something concrete and practical, but forget about everyday gadgets: What's the point of a smartphone or ventilator if the tools and knowledge required for production are still millennia away?[1] Better than a product is an idea. Press fast-forward on humanity's greatest discoveries, and offer a head start on flight, radio or antibiotics. Or you can introduce democracy or promote diplomacy. After all, stable societies advance fastest.

But in a school math exam, you don't get full credit by simply knowing the answer; you have to show your work. In the same fashion, all these options are unfortunately flawed. They rely on a wider infrastructure of knowledge without which they are somewhat meaningless.[2] Human invention takes its own time. There's no skeleton key to progress. Mistakes are also essential: Many important discoveries, from radioactivity to penicillin to the microwave, were made by accident.

Perhaps it would be most sensible to not send anything at all. You have no idea how your information would change history, upsetting delicate power balances in nature or between societies. We have seen how often inventions created with the best intentions are retooled for greed and aggression. Why potentially give the people who happen to find your message extra ammunition?

Another reason to leave the time machine alone: In sending information back to change history, you will probably stop yourself and everyone you know from ever existing. That might be a deal breaker, depending on your outlook.

If you still insist on sending back some knowledge, you'll have to enlist an inter-temporal translation service. Prehistoric humans will struggle with modern English vernacular. So maybe send a favorite painting or piece of music? At least then they'll know that—despite all the unspeakable destruction in store—there will be beauty in that unimaginable future.

Words by Tom Faber

NOTES

1. In 2009, artist Thomas Thwaites tried to create a toaster from scratch—including the extraction of the raw materials necessary to build it. The production of this simple domestic object took nine months and cost £1,187.54. Even then, modern technology was necessary: he used a microwave to smelt the iron ore.

2. Many visionaries have paid a heavy price for being ahead of their time. Hungarian physician Ignaz Semmelweis hit upon (and proved) the importance of handwashing in hospitals in the 1840s, but doctors were insulted by the idea and ignored his advice. He was rejected as an embarrassment, and died in an asylum.

In Season: Arid Art

On cultural deserts.

Left Photograph: *Wind Draperies* by Paul Godard, Namibia, 2005. Right Photograph: *House to Watch the Sunset* by Not Vital, Niger, 2005.

In the Northern Hemisphere, fall can feel like a season of creative withdrawal: Landscapes are stripped back to their earthy skeletons, temperatures fall and our preoccupations take a turn for the domestic. But desert artists have a different way of relating to barren places: not as withered and uninspiring, but as blank canvases for huge works of art. In the 1960s, land artists and light artists—the former working with site-specific sculpture, the latter with natural and artificial illumination—beat a path to the deserts of the American West where they creat-

ed enormous, often permanent works in the arid landscape. Desert art is now found around the world. *House to Watch the Sunset* (pictured below) was built by Swiss artist Not Vital near the desert city of Agadez in Niger. Constructed with traditional adobe bricks, this architectural sculpture sums up much of what makes arid landscapes enticing: They give artists leave to create surprising, poetic interventions with ample space to breathe. Several thousand miles south in Namibia, artist Paul Godard took the surreal potential of desert landscapes further with

his photograph *Wind Draperies* (pictured left)—a digitally altered image of high sand dunes in the area known as the Wind Cathedral. In a culture that increasingly favors experiential art with photographic power, desert interventions are unlikely to lose currency. Indeed, they are arguably what makes Desert X or Burning Man alluring to so many: The latter, essentially a nine-day party in the Nevada desert, is elevated into something more magical by the sight of huge, often humanoid, sculptures rising into the wide-open sky. *Words by Harriet Fitch Little*

Joekenneth Museau

Photographs: Andre D. Wagner

Spoken-word poet and artist Joekenneth Museau started his career from an unusual place: a one-sided rap battle at the age of 11. "I wrote a dis record to Lil Bow Wow and Lil' Romeo called 'Respect Me,'" he recalls with a laugh. He's since turned those first forays into poetry into a career with a large, and expanding, online following. His latest book, *Days After Your Departure*, about the death of his mother, is accompanied by a short film of the same name.

KM: *How did you start incorporating visuals into your work?* **JM:** I believe that for work to touch people in different ways, it needs to be immersive. I was inspired to take the work further, so that a person who may not be interested in sitting with a book can see the film and then become familiar with the book. It makes the work feel more alive. With *Days After Your Departure*, I needed to heal from something that was foreign to me. I needed to go through various mediums to completely explore the feeling of grief. I think that's what art does. It's a vehicle for expressing what's foreign to us, to process it so that we have a greater familiarity with new emotions and help others to get through it as well.

    KM: *What do you think about the term "Instagram poetry"? Do you find it disparaging?* **JM:** I've read some incredible poetry on Instagram. I think Nayyirah Waheed's poetry is phenomenal. Where the conflict comes in is that certain poetry I read on Instagram lacks depth. So I'm kind of in between. I wouldn't like to be called an Instagram poet. I'd like people to discover my work on Instagram and take a deeper dive into what I do with poetry. I don't make my work to live in a box, but I understand the platform. If I'm writing a body of work, I want that to get into the hands of all types of people. I want to make various points of entry for them to read the whole work.

    KM: *What do you hope readers take away from your work?* **JM:** I hope they see some of themselves in my work. I pride myself on being outrageously vulnerable. So in much of my work, I am challenging people to do the same—to confront the ugly parts of themselves in order to reconcile them. I genuinely feel that if we take care of ourselves, if we give attention to our hearts, we, in turn, become better people because we are self-aware. And if we can become better individuals, we become a better community, a better society. It starts from inside and it just spreads wider and wider.

Interview by Kyla Marshell

As part of *Days After Your Departure*, Museau created an exhibition for Dapper Studios in Brooklyn. The installation was a recreation of his childhood home, intended to "animate the nostalgia of my upbringing" and create memories of his mother that weren't related to mourning.

Get Lucky

We have nearly 100 billion neurons in our brain—about the number of stars in our galaxy—and they must all act in a particular way in order for us to exist precisely as we do. Similarly improbable, as Richard Dawkins wrote, "The potential people who could have been here in my place but who will in fact never see the light of day outnumber the sand grains of Arabia." For that sperm to meet that egg, and so forth. We exist and function, literally, by luck. And yet it feels good not to believe in luck. It's comforting to think that someone or something is in strict control. In the 16th century, theologian John Calvin believed "all events are governed by the secret counsel of God." That has long been the basis of most Western religions: You may not know why something is happening, but there's a reason for it. God is working overtime behind the scenes. The contemporary, secular equivalent that gives us a feeling of control is meritocracy—the idea that your rewards match your labors. The truth, of course, is that where and to whom you are born have far greater influence on your life's trajectory than anything you might do. Kylie Jenner is no more of a "self-made billionaire," as *Forbes* dubbed her, than a poor, hardworking person living in a developing country is lazy or inherently undeserving.

But when things go right, it's hard not to want some credit for it. In his commencement address at Princeton a few years back, Michael Lewis described the number of chance encounters it took for him to write and sell his first book, *Liar's Poker*. His path included a random dinner, which had a random encounter with the wife of a man who happened to work for investment bank Salomon Brothers—Lewis' future employer, about which he would write his bestseller. "All of a sudden people were telling me I was a born writer," Lewis said. "This was absurd. Even I could see that there was another, more true narrative, with luck as its theme. What were the odds of being seated at that dinner next to that Salomon Brothers lady? Of landing inside the best Wall Street firm to write the story of the age?" Success, Lewis said, was merely one outcome of a variety of possibilities. "People really don't like to hear success explained away as luck—especially successful people."

As with all things in life, luck is mostly about perspective. Frane Selak, a 90-year-old Croatian—"the world's luckiest man"—began his string of "luck" in 1962 when he survived a train crash between Sarajevo and Dubrovnik. In 1963, on his first-ever plane trip, the emergency exit opened mid-flight, killing 19 people. In 1966, he was in a bus crash, which killed four. In 1970, his car caught on fire and exploded after he'd escaped to safety. In 1973, flames blew through his car's air vents after an oil issue. In 1995, he was hit by a bus. In 1996, driving in the mountains, his car careened over a railing, Selak jumping free in the final moment. Was Selak's a life strung together by great luck (he avoided so much death!) or great misfortune (he came close to death so often!)? Luck is malleable thing. How we perceive it exposes our deepest beliefs. To attribute success to luck is to not only be humble. It's to be realistic. Cosmic fortune works much harder than "hard work" ever could.
Words by Cody Delistraty

On the primacy of chance.

Photograph: Fox Photos / Stringer / Getty Images

Hobbyhorses

In opposition to passive politics.

In his new book, *Politics Is for Power*, Tufts University professor Eitan Hersh makes a provocative argument: Watching cable news, obsessing over the latest scandal—even voting only in presidential elections—is political hobbyism. Instead of engaging with politics as a civic duty, or as a means to change our communities, he says, we treat it like a sport—tune in, do little, rinse, repeat. Here, Hersh offers some ideas on how to break out of passive politics, and spring into action.

KM: *Instead of thinking of politics like a hobby or a sport, how should we think of it?* **EH:** When I think about people doing politics, I think about people working with other people on goals or strategies to influence the government. Maybe they want to get some of their neighbors to vote a certain way or they want to lobby a politician. Most people aren't going to do politics like that; they don't have time. But what's happening is there are a lot of people spending an hour or two a day consuming political news, and arguing, and worrying. The book is all about trying to get people to take the time they're already spending on politics and make it less like a hobby, and more strategic. I talk about power, which is a word that sometimes scares people, but that's what politics is about. It's about convincing people to take some action that they wouldn't otherwise take.

KM: *Is voting an effective way to make change?* **EH:** Voting in every election is doing the bare minimum, and almost everyone is failing at that. People are spending all this time on the news, and then they don't know anything about the politics in their own community. If you ask people why they don't vote in local elections, they'll either say, "That stuff's not important" or "I don't even know who's running." And that's a mistake. If you ask right now which issues people think are important, Democrats might say the environment, or racial equality; Republicans might say economic development, or religious liberty. All of those issues have very clear important things going on at the local level. No one lives in a red or blue bubble when it comes to those things. But people are paying attention to national drama instead.

KM: *Why is it that no seems to understand how important local politics really is?* **EH:** It's work. People are interested in the grandstanding and the fighting [of national politics] because that's the fun part. The details—how government actually works and solves concrete problems—bore them. The politics of getting things done is slow and steady.

KM: *You talk about how liberal white people are particularly bad at engaging effectively. Have you been able to persuade any of them to change?* **EH:** I get emails all the time from white liberals who are like, "You got me." The racial and gender dynamics on this are really clear. The people who are spending the most time community organizing are African Americans, Latinos, and women. The people who are just learning facts about politics, or listening to podcasts are college-educated white men. I want people to say, "I just sent my slate of candidates to 100 people and 10 told me they're going to vote my way." If you have time to spend on politics, that's the conversation I want you to be impressing your friends with.
Interview by Kyla Marshell

Mona Chalabi

On sending spreadsheets viral.

Not long into my interview with data journalist Mona Chalabi, I find myself telling her all about my first heartbreak. It's not what you'd expect from a conversation with someone who spends their time interpreting facts and figures, but Chalabi's interest in drawing out personal stories has become the defining aspect of her work with data. It informs her hand-drawn aesthetic, which combines illustration with data visualization to inject humanity and emotion into statistics.[1]

Chalabi first gained popularity on Instagram while she worked a journalism day job; her colorful data visualizations have since been published in *The New York Times* and *The New Yorker* as well as *The Guardian US*, where she now works as a data editor. She has also created documentaries—one of which, *Vagina Dispatches*, was nominated for an Emmy—and has appeared as a guest on satirical panel shows. Born in London, Chalabi lived in Paris and Jordan before moving to the US in 2014. She spoke to me from her home in New York, surrounded by doodles and graphs.

TF: *Imagine you just received a fresh spreadsheet full of numbers. Do you have a method for how you approach data to find a story?* **MC:** Very often my question is: "Who's affected here?" Once I was looking into a silly story: National Sandwich Day was coming up and I wanted to look at America's favorite sandwich fillings. I downloaded a resource where Americans keep a meticulous food diary for two days. The data is coded, so turkey might be "3A" on the spreadsheet and you're constantly cross-referencing. For some people it might look cold and sterile, but I found this one row that said someone had a glass of milk at 1 p.m. and a cheese sandwich at 4 p.m., and that's all they ate all day. Then you read across and see Hispanic man, 65, recently widowed. I wanted to know more: What's his income status? Is he working? Who is this man? When you come at it with a curiosity about the texture of people's lives, it changes how you approach the data.

TF: *You tackle both "hard" and "soft" subjects in your work. Do you ever find that a difficult balancing act?* **MC:** I see no problem with showing racism one day and something silly the next. It's part of having intimacy with your audience, because that's what real-life relationships are like. With the closest people in my life we'll talk about a friend's suicide attempt and then on that same phone call you'll hear them fart and you laugh about it. That's life.

NOTES

1. Chalabi says that the reason there's a hand-drawn component to her work isn't purely aesthetic; it also helps to convey the imprecision and limitations of all data. "Admitting what I don't know builds trust with the audience," she says.
—

2. Through her dating spreadsheet, Chalabi noticed patterns in her approach. Among them, that she would only go on dates on Monday or Tuesday nights. "Dating was the lowest priority on my list," she explains. "I would never want to give up seeing a friend to go on a date with a stranger."

TF: *How do you choose reliable sources?* **MC:** I often trust government numbers because they're collected by statisticians who are impartial and serve successive governments. People might try to put a spin on the published work but the numbers themselves are solid. And a lot of academic research gives you the opportunity to understand the methodology, which is really valuable. I don't do much work on surveys or opinion polls. I think they're potentially dangerous for our democracy. Saying who's going to win an election before people have gone out to vote is a really fucked up thing to do as a journalist. Our work isn't in prediction, it's accurately depicting the present and the past.

TF: *Do you find the statistics that private companies share to be trustworthy?* **MC:** Private organizations hold incredibly detailed information. Google right now knows more about COVID-19 than any government, in terms of mapping symptoms through searches. These organizations are sitting on vast amounts of data and there's a responsibility to encourage them to share it ethically—which means anonymously.

But often the data comes directly from their communications departments, who have an agenda. There's one simple question you can ask yourself approaching these data sets—have these companies ever shared data that didn't look good for them? Mostly the answer is no. OkCupid is an interesting exception. The founder is a data scientist at heart. He put out blogs that weren't necessarily in OkCupid's best interest, including one that looked at how users are basically racist, and he published it. I have so much respect for that.

TF: *Do you track any data about your personal life which is not for public consumption?* **MC:** Oh yeah, definitely. For ages I kept a spreadsheet on my love life.[2] My column headings included their name, date we met, what number date it was, and a comment section. One comment reads: "He left a chicken bone on the table during dinner and I hated him. Kissed me and I hated it."

TF: *Are there cases where it would be better to be ignorant of the data?* **MC:** It's tricky. Here's an example: The French government forbids collection of data on religion, but Islamophobia is rife there. Imagine you are a 17-year-old Arab kid and you find out that your chances of getting a good job are one in a hundred, while your white peer has got a one-in-twenty chance. What does that do to your self-esteem? So I'm always thinking about the emotional impact my work has, particularly on marginalized communities. There's power in knowing the odds are stacked against you, but it's also hugely disempowering to know you have to work three times as hard.

TF: *It seems especially hard for people from an Arab background, who aren't even given their own category in documents like the American census.* **MC:** I think being Arab has massively informed my understanding of data. I'm never represented in a data set, just like anyone who grows up queer, for example. I know Arabs who check the "White" box and Arabs who check the "Asian" box. If you grow up not fitting the boxes, you know that those boxes are all inherently flawed.

TF: *Are there subjects you'd be hesitant to approach from a data perspective?* **MC:** When people ask me for data to validate somebody's experience, that sets off a red flag. I don't want to tell a queer woman that she's experienced homophobia if she'd prefer to just think somebody gave her a funny look. People should choose how they interpret their experiences, particularly in minority communities where you're constantly being gaslighted.

TF: *I was beaten up outside a gay club when I was 16 and years later I was asked if I'd ever experienced gay-bashing, and I said no. Thinking afterward, I wondered why I didn't want to admit it.* **MC:** Well, both outcomes are shit, right? You either live in a world where people hate you for being queer, or—or what? People are just violent for no apparent reason?

TF: *It's a lose-lose.* **MC:** When I was 14 some guy pissed on me after school. I was in my uniform sitting at the bus stop and this drunk guy came up behind me and called me a "Paki." Then I felt something splash on my feet. At the time I wasn't willing to attribute it to racism, because if you put it down to discrimination, the world becomes a scary place.

TF: *Do you think we would have a better world if we were all aware of what data often shows—the social and cultural currents that shape our thinking and behavior?* **MC:** Definitely. Going back to OkCupid, the data shows people tend to prefer people of their own race. Two groups are consistently unpopular for heterosexual matches: black women, because blackness is perceived as masculine, and Asian men, because Asian-ness is perceived as feminine. Unless you're willing to confront those racist stereotypes, you'd have to conclude there's simply something unattractive about black women or Asian men. So that awareness is really important for self-esteem. For a black woman, how does knowing that data change how you approach the world of dating? Is it depressing to know it's going to be harder for you, or does it make you feel better when you can say: "Yeah, the world's fucking racist, there's nothing wrong with my face."

Interview by Tom Faber

> "I think being Arab has massively informed my understanding of data. If you grow up not fitting the boxes, you know that those boxes are all inherently flawed."

In one visualization that went viral, Chalabi used the stars on the American flag to demonstrate what the country would look like without various minority communities.

Helle Thygesen

The Danish antiques dealer on rare pieces and how to find them.

Photograph: Christian Møller Andersen

Helle Thygesen is a Danish art and antiques dealer. Having grown up in a family that was "very much into art," she studied art history at university and worked at the Copenhagen gallery The Apartment from 2012 to 2014. The following year, she launched her eponymous website, where she sells a handpicked selection of modern and contemporary art and decorative objects. She lives in Copenhagen's leafy northern suburbs.

JC: *How do you work?* HT: I browse online all day, every day. I tend to buy mostly from French and English auction houses. Now that I've been around for about five years I have a very good network of dealers who contact me when they have pieces they think I'll find interesting.

JC: *What kind of pieces are you drawn to?* HT: Well, I like many different things. Abstract paintings. Vintage Picasso posters. Eighteenth-century Japanese wood-engraving prints. But I'd say I specialize in art from the 1920s to the 1970s.

JC: *How would you describe your taste?* HT: There's no question it comes from my father's side of the family. This whole way of mixing antiques with contemporary pieces is very much what I grew up with. My father ran an auction house, my grandparents were collectors and my great-grandfather was the sculptor Einar Utzon-Frank. To me, art was never something I couldn't touch, it was just part of our lives, and that's a good starting point when you're working in this business.

JC: *Can you describe a recent piece you've acquired?* HT: Last week, at a Scottish auction house, I successfully bid on a beautiful set of 19th-century architectural studies in watercolor. Most of my pieces are from the 20th century, so I love it when I find something older that I think my clients will understand and love as well. I think it makes a collection that much more beautiful if you have some older pieces to contrast with the newer ones.

JC: *Do you have any rules for what you buy or sell?* HT: I tend not to buy pieces I've seen elsewhere. I like having pieces you don't just see everywhere.

JC: *Speaking of which, mid-century modern design still casts a long shadow.* HT: Yes—and, speaking as a Dane, it's just such a dominant part of our design DNA and how everybody lives. I have to admit that sometimes when I open a Danish design auction catalog, I can't help but think, "Can this really go on with the same Arne Jacobsen or Hans Wegner? Can people still get excited about it?" At the same time, I recognize its very obvious quality and craftsmanship and the simplicity of the design. So I don't think its place is undeserved, but I do think that it becomes more interesting when you mix it up with more contemporary pieces.

JC: *Since you started out, have you seen more people interested in buying at auction?* HT: Definitely. Within the past five to 10 years, people have really discovered that you can get some fantastic pieces at auction, and perhaps they also recognize that those are pieces they'll probably hold on to forever. A lot of people buying at auction are inspired by pieces they see on websites such as mine and they want to see if they can find them for themselves. That's certainly an incentive for me to find pieces that aren't around that much.

JC: *Has your clientele changed much?* HT: I'm 43, and when I started out, many of my clients were like me, in their late 30s, perhaps having just bought their first home and wanting some nice pieces to fill it with. They've grown up with me. Whereas before they might have looked for a poster, today they might prefer rare ceramics. At the same time, I have a lot of younger clients, people in their mid-to-late 20s who, instead of going and buying four nondescript items, are willing to save up and buy one thing they think, or hope, they will love forever.

JC: *What advice do you give people who want to start collecting art or antiques?* HT: Bargains are hard to come by today because everything is online, but if you put in the time and know a little bit about what you're looking for, it's still possible to find a rare gem. I'd also advise you to read a lot about art history and to establish good relationships with dealers that you know have pieces you like, because all dealers love a passionate client.

JC: *Finally, what's in your own collection?* HT: It's a mix of pieces I inherited from my father, pieces I bought with my husband and pieces I bought myself. It's quite eclectic: like an 18th-century baroque table with a 20th-century French chair. I love the fact that when I look around my home, the reason that each piece is there is that somebody, maybe 100 years ago, loved it enough to take care of it and preserve it for future generations, and then somebody else did the same, and now I'm doing the same.
Interview by James Clasper

Beneath the Rubble

On the appeal of ancient ruins.

Humans are usually disgusted by decay. Evolution has taught us to turn up our noses at sunken pears and moldy biscuits. But when it comes to architecture, we can't get enough of it. People love ruins.

It's an old love. The cultures most commonly associated with ruins—the Greeks and Romans—were fascinated by the broken remains of still more ancient civilizations. When, in turn, celebration of the Greeks and Romans reached a zenith in the 18th and 19th centuries, the fad became so intense that no European country estate was complete without an imitation ruin—manicured ivy on freshly laid plaster.

Large timescales are hard to fathom, and ruins give the mind a sense of history that few other things can. Add to that the strange, intoxicating feeling of being alive in the imagined presence of so many who aren't (think the Parthenon exhaling centuries at dusk). Meditation on transience has a strong allure. Unfortunately, our somber moods don't age half as well as marble. Ruin-love is only ever a step or two ahead of sentimentality. The problem might stem from celebrating a thing's past-ness, rather than the thing itself. Take those Greek statues and temples, so often celebrated for their pristine, unimprovable balance. And yet our image of white marbled bodies is a complete anachronism. Greek sculptures were routinely dyed, painted and gilded when they were made. Ancient Athens would shock us with color if we traveled there. The myth of whiteness in ancient sculpture, fueled in large part by racial bias, was so ingrained that for years curators would scrape off the remnants of dye before displaying them.

Classical ruin-love yearns for a bygone clarity that has decayed into the confusing present. It can still be found in the work of photographer Yves Marchand, for example, and his stunning images of the ruins of Detroit—vast industrial-age theaters, transit hubs and lobbies that have been half-reclaimed by nature. And before you mock those plaster ruins added to 18th-century estates, consider the current fad for exploring more contemporary ruins, like Marisa Scheinfeld's photography of abandoned Catskill resorts, with their rotting paisley wallpapers and caved-in, smoke-stained ceilings. It's a cruel mind that leaves no space for sentiment. And if ruins can help us understand just how short our lives are in the span of history—how little time we have to love and do what we can—then they've done good work. Still, it's worth remembering that those who built them also lived a jumbled, confusing existence. Nothing was ever made in the past, just an earlier present.
Words by Asher Ross

2.

Features

50 — 112

50
Haatepah Clearbear

60
Miyoko Yasumoto

70
Material Girl

78
Vizcaya Gardens

84
At Home With: Nanushka

90
Downsizing

98
*Short Histories
of Nearly Everything*

102
Helen Frankenthaler

HAATEPAH CLEAR—BEAR:

IT'S TRULY *EMPOWERING* TO KNOW WHERE YOU COME FROM.

First, *Haatepah Clearbear* learned about his past. Now the young model is using that knowledge to advocate for Native American futures—and the planet. Words by *Robert Ito* & Photography by *Ben Duggan*

In December 2018, Haatepah Clearbear left his hometown of Pacifica, a sleepy coastal suburb of San Francisco, to come to Los Angeles in the hopes of becoming a model. He was 21. Clearbear had had a bit of success with smaller modeling jobs in the Bay Area, and had been encouraged by Daniel Peddle, a casting director and talent scout, to give it a go with the larger agencies in Southern California. Not long after arriving in town, his finances depleted, Clearbear found himself homeless. "I ran out of money really fast," he says. For a while, he couch surfed at friends' places; other nights, he slept in the parks of East LA.

Many aspiring models and actors who make the pilgrimage to Los Angeles experience similar disappointments. They go home poorer yet hopefully wiser, with tales of hardship, and dreams of what might have been. But for Clearbear, bedding down in LA's public parks was just a temporary setback. Four months after arriving, he signed with the local outpost of Storm Management, the international modeling agency whose clients have included Kate Moss, Cindy Crawford and Cara Delevingne. Soon after, he was doing shoots and ad campaigns for Nike, Uniqlo and Lu-

lulemon. "All my dreams are coming true very fast," he says.

At the same time, Clearbear has been using his newfound visibility to advocate for indigenous rights. On his Instagram page, he writes about colorism in Latino communities ("There's no such thing as a native person that's 'too dark' or 'too light'"); an act of vandalism against indigenous rock art in Utah ("Imagine if the Mona Lisa was graffitied on, the whole world would be crying"); and the lingering legacy of Native American imagery and symbols at US high schools ("We are Sacred People not Mascots"). If the page seems to be evolving with every new post, so too is Clearbear. "My tribes are Kumeyaay, Chichimeca and Coahuiltecan," he says. "I've been trying to learn as much as I can about all of those, because for me, it's truly empowering to know where you come from."

For Clearbear, however, that hasn't always been easy. For years, he says, "I thought I was Mexican. I thought I was Latino, you know?" He's telling me all of this from his father's home in Pacifica, where he's sheltering in place because of the global pandemic, as well as looking after his dad's home while he's away, taking care of the dogs and, at the moment,

doing his own laundry. His family roots are sort of a complicated story, he tells me, with assorted relatives and tribes and events that only came to light after Clearbear turned 18. He's still learning details about them now. Even so, a lot of his past remains unknown, and is likely to stay that way. "There's so much to tell you!" he says. "I feel like I don't want to overwhelm you, but there's a lot." Let me hear it, I tell him. The guy is 22, after all. How much could there be? Okay, he says, pausing to collect his thoughts. "If you need me to rephrase anything, or repeat something back, just let me know."

Clearbear and his twin brother, Nyamuull, were born in Santa Clara County on January 6, 1998, and given up for adoption soon after. When they were one, they were adopted by two dads, both white. "We were always looked at by our family as the black sheep, because we looked different than them," he recalls. That difference sparked a desire in both boys to find out who and what they were, and where they came from.

One father was a firefighter with the San Francisco Fire Department, and supported Clearbear's quest to discover his roots. Although Clearbear grew up thinking he was Latino, he somehow knew that he and his brother were also Native American—"I've always been a visibly indigenous person," he says—so one of his fathers began taking him to powwows and encouraging him to learn more about Native cultures. His other father was less understanding. "He would straight up tell me, 'You're not Native, you're Middle Eastern. You're probably mixed with Arab.' And I'd ask my dad, and he'd be like, 'Are you taking crazy pills? You boys are at least half to three-fourths Native.'"

When Clearbear was 17, his more understanding father died of lung cancer. The other was broken by the death of his life partner of 25 years, and took it out on the boys. "He became a lot more cold and mean about it," Clearbear says. "After that happened, he'd say some racist, mean things to us at the dinner table. He'd say, 'You know you're not a wetback, right? You know you're not a drunken Indian, right?' He was just saying it to be antagonizing."

At 18, Clearbear went looking for his biological family. He soon discovered that he had an uncle living nearby, in neighboring Santa Clara. "He nearly had a heart attack when me and my brother told him who we were," Clearbear says. When Clearbear asked about his racial background and whether he was indigenous, his uncle told him yes, we're from Mexico, and we have indigenous roots. The next day, he was meeting family members in nearby San Jose. Unbeknownst to him, Clearbear had been living amid aunts and uncles and cousins his entire life.

He soon discovered, however, that his biological father had died when Clearbear was around five or six. A member of the Kumeyaay tribe, his father had lived in Ensenada, Mexico, but left his family and community, Clearbear says, "to become a gangbanger."

Learning about his biological father only heightened his growing interest in his people and culture. Clearbear became involved with organizations including the Student Kouncil of Intertribal Nations (SKINS) at San Francisco State University, and the American Indian Movement West. Before long, he had created his own group, the Indigenous Alliance Movement. Meeting up with other indigenous people and groups fueled his interest in environmental issues, the climate crisis in particular. "It's something you can't avoid, being a Native," he says. "All indigenous people across the Americas have that one thing in common: trying to work in balance with nature."

At home, however, life had become intolerable. "Me and my brother were in and out of the house, homeless, because we just couldn't take the kind of ugliness that was being thrown in our face," Clearbear says. LA offered both a respite from a bad situation and

At LA's Climate March in 2019, Clearbear performed a water song and marched with a sign around his neck that read "The world is changed by your action not your opinion."

Clearbear's early success as a model was aided by the fact that he already saw fashion as an important statement of identity.

the promise of better things to come. After signing with Storm LA, Clearbear became a full-time model, going on all-night shoots for Lululemon, and appearing in Uniqlo ads alongside his brother. "We were up on the billboards a couple months, and everyone saw them in the Bay Area," he says. "All my aunties. They're not actually my aunties, but in a Native way, we call an older woman who's almost like family, 'auntie.' And they were like, hey, we saw you guys on the billboards! We're so proud of you. It felt good to hear that."

Last September, Clearbear spoke at a climate change protest in Los Angeles as a representative of the International Indigenous Youth Council, and performed a water song taught to him by one of his Navajo elders. "It's a song you sing to give thanks to the water," he says. "You're giving thanks to the Earth, and to the water that sustains all of us." He's also participated in Native ceremonies in Northern California, where concerns about the environment go hand in hand with indigenous issues. "The indigenous spirituality is to protect the Earth, to work with the Earth," he says. "Not to try to kill the Earth or use it for all of its resources, but to work with it rather than against it."

And in November, Clearbear participated in an event honoring the 50th anniversary of the occupation of Alcatraz, one of the watershed moments of the Native American civil rights movement. In 1969, more than 70 activists sailed out to Alcatraz Island—the notorious former prison home of George "Machine Gun Kelly" Barnes and Al Capone—with the intent of "purchasing" the territory in the name of their group, which called itself the Indians of All Tribes (the group offered $24 worth of glass beads and red cloth, the same amount Dutch merchants paid for Manhattan Island in 1626). According to the 1868 Treaty of Fort Laramie, unused federal lands could be claimed by Native Americans, and the members of the group intended to do just that. The occupation ended 19 months later, in June 1971.

But the anniversary that Clearbear attended marked the protest's beginnings, when movement heroes like Richard Oakes, a young Mohawk activist and steelworker, and the author and poet John Trudell, the group's spokesperson, first made landfall. Clearbear joined Native activists and some of the original occupiers at the gathering, which attracted members of tribes from throughout California and beyond. "There were indigenous representatives from all over the country, and other countries as well," Clearbear remembers. "That was one of the most beautiful experiences of my whole entire life."

Lately, things have slowed a bit because of COVID-19, but not by much. An assignment with Calvin Klein was put on hold during the lockdown, as well as talks to appear in a film about Joaquin Murrieta, aka "The Robin Hood of the West," a legendary Mexican outlaw and gang leader who was allegedly killed and beheaded during the height of the California gold rush. But the two brothers are keeping busy. Clearbear is planning to travel to Colombia in the next few weeks to plant and pick cacao with members of the Arhuaco tribe. His brother, he says, is going to meet with members of the Kumeyaay tribe, their biological father's people, in Ensenada, and plans to bring face masks and other essential goods. As for his adoptive father, Clearbear has made peace with him, after the estrangement that sent him and his brother down to LA in the first place.

Clearbear continues to advocate for indigenous rights on his Instagram page. In recent posts, he's railed against the murder rate of indigenous people in Utah; spoken out about the imprisonment of indigenous youth and families in US-run detention centers; and called out Jair Bolsonaro, whom he calls the "openly racist president of Brazil," for trying to send evangelical missionaries to the indigenous peoples of the Amazon.

"If I were to say all this stuff that I'm talking about in any other country, I would definitely be murdered," he says. "There was an indigenous activist trying to save the butterflies in Mexico, and he was murdered. Just for trying to save the butterflies, man! And he was murdered for that." That sort of sacrifice, Clearbear says, is not for him. He loves life too much, for one thing. And he has too much he wants to do and see. He'll continue the struggle, he says, "but in a smart way, where I'm not gonna die, of course. I'd rather live for my people than die for them."

"The indigenous spirituality is to work with the earth rather than against it."

Clearbear has previously spoken about his ambition to learn silversmithing at the Institute of American Indian Arts in Santa Fe, New Mexico. Other long-term possibilities include opening a martial arts gym or becoming an actor.

Flower Arranging:
Miyoko Yasumoto

In her Parisian atelier, *Miyoko Yasumoto* makes an unfrivolous case for floristry. Words by *Annick Weber* & Photography by *Luc Braquet*

Not everyone would want to live in their work space, but in Miyoko Yasumoto's case, it's an appealing setup. "I live amid flowers," the Japanese French floral designer says, sitting in her loft-style home in the Parisian suburb of Aubervilliers. All around her are colorful floral arrangements, some finished and ready to go to her clients, others still waiting for that final touch—a bit of foliage, say, or a showpiece bloom. On the wall hangs a half-completed weaving she's making with pressed wildflowers and linen, while behind her, a floor-to-ceiling window opens onto a leafy courtyard.

Yasumoto worked as a designer before retraining in floristry at Paris' École des Fleuristes in 2016. She established her floral atelier, Une Maison dans les Arbres, in 2018, after a stint running Paris' first dried flower boutique in a corner of L'Officine Universelle Buly's Marais shop. Though she still has a penchant for dried bouquets, she now incorporates seasonal cut flowers and other greenery from small local producers, bridging the gap between the ephemeral and the lasting, the fresh and the frozen-in-time. She finds inspiration as much in the landscapes of the southwest of France—where she spent her childhood summers—as she does in the minimalism of ikebana, the Japanese art of sculptural flower arrangement. The resulting bouquets look organic, as if swept up from a wildflower meadow.

AW: *Forgive me if this is like asking a parent to choose between their children, but do you have a favorite flower?* **MY:** No, I don't, but I find the smell of a garden rose extraordinary. It's of personal significance to me. A friend offered me one just after the Paris attacks of 2015, in which I lost a colleague. I had been working as an art director for 20 years and suddenly found myself in this traumatic situation, questioning my life. I realized that my job at the design agency had disconnected me from my inner self, and so I decided it was time for a change; it was time to pursue what makes me happy.

AW: *How did you decide what that was exactly?* **MY:** Everyone has to work it out for themselves. The smell of that garden rose triggered something inside me. I had the feeling it brought the real me back to the surface—things were finally aligned. Nature gave me so much comfort in those difficult times.

AW: *Why did you choose floristry in particular?* **MY:** There were many nature-related professions that interested me, but I didn't want to study for too long. After all those years in front of a computer, I knew I wanted to move on to working with something tangible fairly quickly. I received my

Yasumoto dries flowers so that her winter arrangements can be more sustainable. During lockdown, this has become a popular hobby for many people.

diploma [in 2016] and started as a freelance floral designer a year later.

AW: *Has the profession turned out to be what you expected it to be?* **MY:** It has certainly made me realize that I wasn't alone in seeking solace in nature. During the [coronavirus] lockdown, I did fresh flower deliveries because so many people were dreaming of having a bit of nature at home. I arranged these bouquets around aromas, using mint, verbena, lemongrass and more traditional elements such as peonies. Smells are so powerful; they can overshadow any anxiety and negative thoughts

AW: *You basically recreated your garden rose moment for others.* **MY:** Exactly. It makes the reptilian part of our brain feel safe.

AW: *Was there anything that surprised you about floristry?* **MY:** I wasn't expecting the flower industry to be so closely connected to hyperconsumerism and its environmental impacts. In my eyes, it's nonsense to make roses come all the way from Kenya in February—and yet it's totally normal, as I learned during my placements in various Parisian flower shops. That's when I knew that traditional floristry was not my thing.

AW: *Were you worried you'd chosen the wrong path?* **MY:** No, but I realized I had to develop a voice of my own. You shouldn't need masses of exotic blooms to create something beautiful.

AW: *But what about winter when there are hardly any seasonal flowers around?* **MY:** I turned to dried flowers for this very reason. They resonated with me ethically and aesthetically speaking. They're in rhythm with the seasons, giving you a palette of plants to work with year-round. I also like the nostalgia they evoke, especially when mixed with fresh flora or sheaths of grass. Who doesn't have childhood memories of pressing flowers and keeping them as a souvenir of the summer holidays?

AW: *What do those memories look like for you?* **MY:** It makes me think of my summers spent at my grandparents' in Poitou, in the southwest of France, where I still go to pick many of the flowers I work with. There were flowers everywhere: in my grandfather's garden and in the fields around the house. We would go for long walks and come back with bouquets of fresh-picked wildflowers, herbs and grasses.

AW: *Do you think children are natural-born florists?* **MY:** When you're a child you find everything beautiful—a few blossoms here, some leaves there, everything is possible. This spontaneity leads to magnificent results.

AW: *As an adult these things are suddenly much more difficult. Why is that?* **MY:** Because we no longer approach it like a child. When I start a floral arrangement with a particular vision in mind, I usually struggle to get there. The most interesting work happens when letting go of control; that's when emotions can come through. Ikebana has taught me a lot about expressing my feelings through my arrangements, like you would do when writing a haiku poem. I'm no ikebana master, but I'm interested in the general principles.

AW: *Don't the strict rules of ikebana get in the way of working intuitively?* **MY:** Don't get me wrong, you certainly need to be very concentrated. Ikebana was performed by samurai to mentally prepare prior to going into battle; it's a form of meditation. But, similar to the bouquets we used to make as children, everything has a place in this art: the budding, blooming and fading flower, as well as the greenery around it. It's very poetic and a huge inspiration.

AW: *Is there such a thing as a failed composition?* **MY:** I don't think so. I teach floral arranging ateliers to students and have never seen anyone disappointed. Nor have I seen two students create the same arrangement.

AW: *What if the colors don't match? Or the flowers and textures?* **MY:** I believe there's no ready-made formula for what works and what doesn't. Charles Baudelaire said that "the beautiful is always bizarre" and it's true: There's a lot of beauty in the bizarre as it reveals the singularity of the maker. It gives an insight into their heart.

"You shouldn't need masses of exotic blooms to create something beautiful."

Yasumoto's arrangements use grasses native to her family home in southwestern France, including meadow fescue, foxtail and *Stipa pennata*.

Traditional French bouquets look more conservative than those Yasumoto creates. Custom dictates you use no more than three flower species in one tonal shade.

MATERIAL GIRL

The most interesting people, stories and haircuts all have layers. This fall, so does your wardrobe. Photography by Luc Braquet & Styling by Camille-Joséphine Teisseire

Above and Previous Spread: Noémie wears a suit by Acne Studios, a vest by Dries Van Noten, a shirt by Nina Ricci, a scarf by Eric Bompard, a sweatshirt worn as a turban by American Vintage, a hat by Laurence Bosslon and a scarf by Charvet. Left: She wears a dress by Ann Demeulemeester, a brooch by Louis Vuitton, a hat by Laurence Bosslon, a scarf by Samsøe & Samsøe, a sleeve worn as a turban by Undercover and a silk scarf by Charvet.

Above: Noémie wears a coat by Maison Margiela, a coat and a scarf by Uniqlo and two scarves by Eric Bompard. Left: She wears a dress by Arthur Avellano, trousers by Haider Ackermann, a coat by Max Mara, a scarf by Uniqlo, a jacket worn as a headscarf by Haider Ackermann, a hat by Laurence Bossion and a scarf by Charvet.

Noémie wears a poncho by Dries Van Noten, pants by Annakiki, a scarf by Eric Bompard, a turban by Maison Michel and a silk scarf by Charvet.

VIZCAYA

GAR—

A garden once dismissed as a stylistic mishmash now conjures nostalgia for an impossible place.
Words by Cody Delistraty & Photography by Steven Brooke

DENS

Born on November 12, 1859 to one of the wealthiest families in America, James Deering never had the charisma of his father, a businessman and investor who snapped up thousands of acres of land in the then underdeveloped western United States. William Deering had made a fortune when he acquired a farm equipment manufacturer and implemented a technology that allowed for harvesting an acre of grain in an hour—increasing both the value of the business and of his land investments.

James, William's younger son, suffered from anemia and was described by his contemporaries, as recounted in the 2012 film *The Light Club of Vizcaya: A Women's Picture*, as "colorless, meticulous, pedestrian, sedate, dyspeptic, proper, fastidious." He was considered a "lifelong bachelor," likely code for gay, and, as often as he threw parties and moved in large social circles, he seemed forever ill at ease.

"I don't think he was really comfortable with his guests," said the actress Lillian Gish in an interview that featured in the film. Gish described an April evening at Deering's Villa Vizcaya on Biscayne Bay in Miami, when the fireflies were out and they'd just returned from a gondola ride. Upon

returning to dry land all Deering wanted to do was watch a movie about "microbes and germs." "Can you imagine that?" said Lish. "I had the impression that he was a man who wanted to have beauty around him in his house and gardens, but that he didn't know what to do with it."

Deering might not have known "what to do with" beauty quite as Lish wanted, but he had a knack for creating it: The Villa Vizcaya is one of the most stunning villas and gardens in the United States. It's arguably even more impressive than its better-known kin—the Breakers in Newport, Rhode Island, and the Hearst Castle in San Simeon, California. (Though Vizcaya may be less of a name brand, it has appeared in a number of movies, including *Ace Ventura: Pet Detective, Any Given Sunday* and *Iron Man 3*. It was also used by Ronald Reagan to receive Pope John Paul II in 1987 and by Bill Clinton for his First Summit of the Americas in 1994.)

Constructed between 1914 and 1923, the Villa Vizcaya is surrounded by roughly 50 acres of gardens. They draw predominately from French and Italian Renaissance styles while incorporating the plant life of southern Florida's

"I don't know of any other garden intended to induce melancholia."

Vizcaya's waterfront position makes it vulnerable; researchers believe surrounding sea levels have risen a foot since it was constructed.

subtropical ecology, like palms and philodendrons. There is Cuban limestone stonework, and the villa's architecture—much of which looms over the indoor gardens and courtyards—combines the Baroque with Mediterranean Revival architecture. "Turn-of-the-century grand gardens were generally quite formal and symmetrical, with matching borders and often a water feature in the center—pergolas and arbors were much in evidence," says Page Dickey, a garden designer and author of books including *Outstanding American Gardens*. Vizcaya is nothing like this. It is an aesthetic jumble, what some critics at the time called "a laughable pastiche."

But most experts today admire Deering for the singularity of his vision. *In Vizcaya: An American Villa and its Makers*, authors Laurie Olin and Witold Rybczynski describe it as a "Gilded Age triumph." "All of these ideas are molded together as a pastiche of Italian Renaissance, Italian Baroque and French Re-

naissance garden styles," says Ian Simpkins, deputy director of horticulture and urban agriculture at the Vizcaya Museum and Gardens. "This is all united through a very American idea—that we can take something, adapt it to our own uses and make it better."

A trio of designers worked for Deering to create Vizcaya. Deering's friend Paul Chalfin, who'd trained as a painter in Italy, traveled with him throughout Europe; together they bought up pieces of beautiful villas for Vizcaya, from ceiling murals to doors. While in Italy, they met Diego Suarez, "a 25-year-old gardening dilettante who became involved in the project more or less by accident," according to Rybczynski; and, on a trip through New York, Chalfin introduced Deering to F. Burrall Hoffman, a failed painter turned Beaux-Arts architect.

Chalfin, though, was always the key puzzle piece, "responsible for 90% of the beauty" of Villa Vizcaya, writes Rybczynski. "He appeared to be of singular, laser-

like focus and took on this enormous project while remaining focused on detail," Simpkins says of Chalfin. "Without that, Vizcaya would not be nearly as elaborate and would not sing in harmony as it does now, despite pulling its influence from a wide range of sources."

Vizcaya has undergone a number of challenges since its completion. The Great Miami Hurricane of 1926 destroyed much of the gardens and some features, including the rose garden, were never rebuilt. In 1971, there was a robbery, in which three jewel thieves stole artworks and silver. Time itself has taken its toll, too. "Trees grew out of scale, things fell apart or disappeared—pretty much the type of attrition you'd expect from a garden that was not particularly well maintained," says Simpkins. In the 1980s, a roof was added over the courtyard to better preserve fabrics and furniture.

Since 2008, when the National Trust for Historic Preservation listed Vizcaya as one of America's eleven most endangered historic

places, there's been an increased effort to restore the gardens. Because of Deering's anemia, doctors advised him to live in a warm climate and to be in the sun as often as possible. At Vizcaya, he tended to his gardens and boated (he had three yachts.) A Latin quote is inscribed in the villa: "Take the gifts of the hour. Put serious things aside." But the experience of being in the gardens is ultimately not one of hedonism; it is, rather, evocative of nostalgia and melancholy.

The gardens have manifold influences—Italy, France, the 17th through 20th centuries. They are a time machine, a flip-book of eras and possibilities. Like an impossible bouquet, they cannot all be had at once. Walking through them is to experience a certain sadness. Its beauty must be concocted. It cannot exist in nature.

"This garden isn't unique in expressing its nostalgia for another place and time," says Simpkins, "[but] I don't know of any other garden whose creator intended to induce melancholia."

"*This is a very American idea—that we can take something and make it better.*"

At Home With:
Nanushka

Meet the bold couple who took their Budapest brand global. Words by *Laura Rysman* & Photography by *Zoltan Tombor*

Amid the churning tides of fashion, designers come and go in droves, all dreaming of inspiring the way we dress. The odds caution against it. I, for one, spent years attempting to forge an existence as a jewelry designer. "Many are called," my father would warn me in his slowest, most ominous drawl; "few are chosen." He was discouraging. He was also frustratingly correct.

What buoys the winning designers to a place in our wardrobes? Sandra Sandor, founder of the audaciously successful Budapest-based brand Nanushka, was raised on a rallying message. Her mother had launched one of the first privately operated lines of children's clothing in Communist Hungary, defying some fairly perilous odds under a regime that discouraged such aspirations. Sandra started her own women's clothing line in 2005—immediately after graduating from the London College of Fashion, forgoing the customary internship with an established designer and resisting the pull of one of the world's fashion capitals.

"I was 22 years old, and I was quite brave actually," Sandor tells me with a smile. "London was tempting, but I felt I could be based in Budapest and grow an international brand as a sort of cultural mission for Hungary," she says. Her confidence sounds like a wonderful place to be. Nanushka became known for designs that are flamboyant yet contemporary, often tailored into crisp, original silhouettes. But they are also pieces designed to outlast seasonal trends.

Sandor is speaking on a video call from a country house outside Budapest. She shows me around her rural lodgings—a canopy bed under a pitched wood ceiling, an expanse of grass outside, shaded by a fulsome oak tree—but her wonky countryside Wi-Fi reveals only impressionist dabs of colored pixels. On the adjacent computer window, Peter Baldaszti, her fiancé and CEO, tunes in. Broadcasting against a stark white wall in the Nanushka office in Budapest, he squints into the camera. "Sandra always knew how to design to make customers happy," he tells me. To succeed, "she just needed the structure to empower her creativity with the right framework and team structure."

"At the beginning, my mom provided a safe space for me," Sandor explains. She is talking both literally and figuratively. Nanushka, baptized in honor of Sandor's childhood nickname (she mispronounced her own name as "Nany," which became the diminutive Nanushka), was launched from her mother's garage, where the designer knocked together a showroom and office. She spent the first five years as her own saleswoman. "I love the act of selling. I loved to be on the shop floor. Maybe my mom taught me this, but I think it's just something that's in both of us. I'm a little merchant deep inside," she says.

"Pleather" (plastic leather) has typically been derided by the fashion industry as a cheap substitute. Rebranded as "vegan leather," however, the material has become a popular choice for ethically conscious consumers. A 2017 vegan leather puffer jacket helped Nanushka become a globally recognized brand.

"We were close to bankruptcy a couple of times. I had to sell my apartment."

Sandor's vision for her clothing line was expansive. For her mother, Hungary was sufficiently vast; Sandor, born in 1982, was young enough to experience the world not from behind the Iron Curtain but from Hungary's new position as part of a globalized society. "I always saw Nanushka as an international brand," she says. And she always believed in its success. "It was challenging—we were close to bankruptcy a couple of times. I had to sell my apartment in the 2008 crisis. But I was always optimistic." When Baldaszti came into her life, Nanushka had been leaking money for years, and sales were still mostly limited to Hungary despite Sandor's worldwide ambitions. He became her boyfriend in 2013, then, in 2016, her CEO and business partner.

"With all the failures I've gone through, I've managed to gain some business acumen," Baldaszti deadpans, fingering the collar of his black turtleneck. "I've been an entrepreneur ever since I was 19." Nanushka marked his first stint in fashion, after career leaps from tech to hospitality, yet he was sharp-eyed in his plans for the brand: investment, expansion, more investment, more expansion.

"It was," he pauses, and furrows his dark eyebrows, "terribly difficult to drum up investment at first. I had never worked with a professional investor before." It took 15 months, but he injected about $3 million into the brand in partnership with a venture capital firm, GB & Partners. In addition to cash, they provided "a big brother eye watching over you," as Baldaszti describes it, which forced the business to incorporate detailed reporting, firm deadlines and structure. "Emerging designers need partners," says Baldaszti. "They need investors and [wholesale and PR] agencies, and it's crucial to be open-minded and learn from these people. Being successful in fashion is a huge team effort."

Sandor and Baldaszti had hoped to get married this year; instead, the pandemic has postponed the festivities to next summer. Still, the couple has much to celebrate with Nanushka already: The brand has a loyal following online and is stocked by high-profile international retailers—Bergdorf Goodman, Saks Fifth Avenue, Browns, Net-a-Porter and Mytheresa among them. It brought in $23.5 million last year, 25 times more than when Baldaszti first came on board. Nanushka added

menswear in 2018, and launched a flagship shop in Budapest in 2017, followed by a second location in New York's SoHo neighborhood last fall.

But 2020, which marks the brand's 15th anniversary, and the couple's seventh, is tumbling fashion giants and fledglings alike. For Sandor and Baldaszti, however, optimism and expansion continue to be the order of the day. As we speak, their New York store is still shuttered for the lockdown, and the fashion press is mourning the likely doom of physical retail, but the pair discusses bright plans for the inauguration of a London shop in September. The location would host a showroom, office and, on the top floor, a Nanushka-branded hotel room. A big step. A big investment in risky times.

Even as they're working on international expansion, Sandor is also focused on sustainability, which has guided her since the brand's founding. As she's become more educated about the environmental impact of the fashion industry, and had more options open to the company as it has grown, she says she's been "trying to improve in little steps each season."

How to pair the contrary goals of growth and sustainability? There is no creative success in fashion without capitalist expansion. Yet among the new generation of designers, many are trumpeting sustainability, longevity and pared-down essentialism. "It's not black and white," Sandor says. "It's tough because sustainability is quite important to me, but aesthetically I'm a maximalist." Increased sustainable offerings have somewhat helped her settle between the two. Nanushka uses organic cotton and recycled cashmere. Its most popular designs have been separates in vegan leather—a polyurethane-based alternative to animal hides. The material comes with its own polluting problems but, as Sandor points out, it has one-third of the environmental impact of cow leather.

"Durability and functionality are values that, for me, are equal to beauty," she says, her features still aglow with country sunlight. "In terms of sustainability, design has a very responsible role." Sandor thinks about what the future holds and says, "After the pandemic, we'll all be craving more physical contact and physical experiences. This period just reassured me about the importance of following our own values."

Unable to travel during lockdown, architects Salem Charabi & Rasmus Stroyberg decided to recreate a favorite building. Photography by Christian Møller Andersen

Designed by Sverre Fehn for the Venice Biennale in 1962, the Nordic Pavilion was hailed as a masterpiece of airy mid-century design.

Charabi and Stroyberg recreated the pavilion in their Copenhagen studio using a 1:20 scale.
The model was made using oak, mahogany, limestone gravel and gouache, and fitted with a tiny oil painting by Anton Funck.

Essay:

Short Histories
of Nearly Everything

Words by Debika Ray

The nonfiction charts were once dominated by celebrity memoirs and self-help books. Now, they look more like a college reading list; from the history of man in Sapiens to the history of economics in Capital, the bestsellers of the last decade have taken a turn for the intellectual. Debika Ray looks at how global uncertainty, social media overload and the TED Talks juggernaut all contributed to the rise of the "brainy book."

In June 2018, publishing trade magazine *The Bookseller* reported a "dramatic shift" in the UK thirst for nonfiction, with the celebrity biographies that had previously dominated the market falling away in favor of "more intelligent" titles. Over the previous five years, books that tackled big questions in politics, economics, history and medicine had seen an unprecedented boom. The most notable of these is *Sapiens: A Brief History of Humankind* by Yuval Noah Harari, which has sold hundreds of thousands of copies worldwide since its 2014 English-language publication date. *The Bookseller*'s charts and data editor, Kiera O'Brien, told *The Guardian* that it was rare for such books to have this kind of longevity. "Non-fiction tends to be very much of its time," she said. "Now it feels like we've broken that mould."

Sapiens isn't alone: *Thinking, Fast and Slow* by Daniel Kahneman; *Why I'm No Longer Talking to White People About Race* by Reni Eddo-Lodge; *Quiet: The Power of Introverts in a World that Can't Stop Talking* by Susan Cain; *Invisible Women: Exposing Data Bias in a World Designed for Men* by Caroline Criado Perez; *Capital in the Twenty-First Century* by Thomas Piketty—these brainy books have been as much a part of the recent conversation as many landmark works of fiction.

Of course, works of nonfiction have made a splash in the past: Charles Darwin's *On the Origin of Species* (1859) captured the attention of the general public and, last century, books like Stephen Hawking's *A Brief History of Time* (1988) and Rachel Carson's *Silent Spring* (1962) made their authors into household names.

Nonetheless, until the past few decades, novels occupied center stage. "In the post–World War II era people turned to characters in fiction for narratives of independence and personal liberation that would give them permission to move forward in life," says Wendy S. Walters, author of *Multiply/Divide: On the American Real and Surreal*, who has taught nonfiction at Columbia University and other major institutions. Nonfiction, she says, "was relegated to the job of historical material and biographies of heroic figures." Now, the nonfiction book charts are populated with diverse titles intended for popular consumption.

"There's definitely a bigger interest in the smart end of nonfiction," says Jamie Joseph, editorial director at nonfiction publisher Ebury, which recently published *The Volunteer* by Jack Fairweather, the story of a Polish soldier who infiltrated Auschwitz and *Letters from an Astrophysicist*, a *New York Times* bestseller by Neil DeGrasse Tyson. "If you went back five or 10 years, you would see YouTube stars, celebrity biographies. It would look like quite a different list." The most popular nonfiction titles today have a fresh angle and an authorly or journalistic approach. "People aren't just looking for dispatches from the front line of the field—there are academic books out there for that," Joseph says. "What they are looking for is a big human story and a compelling narrative."[1] He points to *The Dance of Life: Symmetry, Cells and How We Become Human* (2019), which integrates the emotive personal story of one of its authors, Magdalena Zernicka-Goetz, who received news of an abnormal pregnancy before giving birth to a healthy baby.

Joseph says that the best person to write such a book isn't always the primary expert in the field, but rather someone who can connect to an audience. "The ideal writer is saying something new or a bit controversial without being a crank. They need to be willing to stick their neck out, but have the authority to do it."

What is it about the current moment that is drawing people to these books? The obvious answer is that the world has become increasingly complex and chaotic, and we are conscious of how little we know. Popular science and history books help make sense of abstract but important ideas that affect modern life. Joseph puts it bluntly: "As the world has gone to shit, people are turning to nonfiction to give them some guidance."

Walters notes that consuming nonfiction may be a way of equipping ourselves with crucial information to defend against challenges. "Science has been historically touted as an authority, so when people read a science book, that's an opportunity for them to garner their own authority, especially on issues that might be related to their own experience." This perhaps explains why *Sapiens* has apparently been embraced by the tech crowd of Silicon Valley—an industry that has come to dominate the world.[2]

But most recently, Walters has seen a shift away from that and toward books about the environment: She points to *The Sixth Extinction: An Unnatural History* by Elizabeth Kolbert (2014) and the "shocking success" of Robin Wall Kimmerer's *Braiding Sweetgrass: Indigenous Wisdom, Scientific Knowledge, and the Teachings of Plants* (2013), a book about botany from a Native American perspective. "There seems to be a move toward the human species being decentered and the natural world repositioned as the heroic character in the story."

It's impossible to ignore the fact that this surge is happening in a supposedly post-truth world—one in which, we're told, expertise is denigrated and religion is experiencing a resurgence. Does the growing popularity of nonfiction speak to a revival of interest in more concrete certainties?

It's worth remembering that these works of supposed fact are themselves subjective—the history and science we read (in popular as well as academic texts) are the writer's interpretation and the information they have decided to present to support their thesis, as well the choice of publishers as to who to give a platform. Academia itself, Walters points out, is subject to the influence of private funders and lobbyists. "There can be an outsized influence of certain

---

NOTES

1. Rutger Bregman's new book follows this formula. In *Humankind: A New History of Human Nature*, the Dutch historian tells a story of humanity as fundamentally "friendly, peaceful and healthy." Reviewers generally praised the book for its optimism but faulted it for papering over the cracks in order to tell a good story. As Siddharth Venkataramakrishnan put it in the *Financial Times*, "Labelling his central thesis as a 'mind-bending drug' feels more than a little unnecessary."
—
—

2. In a 2018 interview with *The New York Times*, Harari appeared confused and displeased by his own popularity in Silicon Valley given that he believes its ethos is undermining democracy. "[Maybe] my message is not threatening to them, and so they embrace it," he said.

corporate or technological interests and it can be hard for scientists to get academic positions if their interests aren't clearly aligned to those of funders." The brainy books that make it to market are also dictated by the demands of the audience, and people invariably want something easily digestible—a ready meal that sates our hunger for new information but also makes us feel good. It's a formula that resembles that of the TED Talk, which epitomizes the way in which we consume serious information in the digital age. Some of these books have been criticized for simplifying and glamorizing complex, often dull, subjects with sweeping, inspiring narratives and surprising statistics and assertions. "*Sapiens* feels like a study-guide summary of an immense, unwritten text—or, less congenially, like a ride on a tour bus that never stops for a poke around the ruins," journalist Ian Parker wrote in a 2020 profile of Harari in *The New Yorker*.

"The ideal writer is saying something new or a bit controversial without being a crank. They need to be willing to stick their neck out, but have the authority to do it."

Joseph sheds some light on how the kinds of books people are looking to read shape what is published: He receives many pitches about the increasingly important field of artificial intelligence, for example. "But it's hard to make people care about it because it doesn't feel very human—it's abstract and scary. Important, not attractive. The books that work best are typically those with a bit of a positive angle and that are reassuring," he says.

Walters speculates that the popularity of these nonfiction books is exposing the fault lines in society we repeatedly encounter across the world at the moment—the divide between adjacent communities with different values. "Some people are satisfied to rely on narratives that are unsubstantiated by data, while others feel the opposite way and are very much bolstered by evidence and facts and make their decisions accordingly," she says. And of course, many of us hold competing desires within us: We are also torn between our simultaneous urges to run toward or run away from reality. "As well as this rise in interest in serious ideas, we're also seeing a massive trend towards escapist fiction," Joseph says. "People either want to really understand what's going on or they want to run away from it—I think most of us have a bit of a both."

Archive:
Helen Frankenthaler

On the legacy of artist Helen Frankenthaler—a self-described "square" and the pioneer of the freewheeling, feeling-focused Color Field movement.

Above: Frankenthaler in front of *Interior Landscape* (in progress, 1964) in her studio at East 83rd Street and Third Avenue, New York, in 1964. Right: Frankenthaler behind *Inner Edge* (turned on its side, 1966) in her New York studio in 1966. Previous: Frankenthaler at her studio in Provincetown, Massachusetts, in the summer of 1968 with the paintings *Summer Banner* hanging upside down on the wall, *Spices* in her hands and, in the foreground, *Summer Core*

Helen Frankenthaler changed the course of American abstractionism with her free-flowing color fields and built "a bridge between Pollock and what was possible," as one visitor to her studio gushed afterward. But while her canvases sang with color, daring and invention, she lived her own life strictly within the lines. Words by *Tim Hornyak*

There's an early photograph by *Life* magazine's Gordon Parks of artist Helen Frankenthaler in a corner of her studio, with the walls and floor covered in her outsized canvases, large washes of blues, grays, pinks and browns. Dressed in a blouse and skirt, legs tucked under her, Frankenthaler has a faraway, dreamy expression and almost looks like a mermaid in an undersea fantasy. It's an image that symbolizes the intense, immersive quality of Frankenthaler's paintings, drawing the viewer into an irresistible maelstrom of color. "People say to me, 'How do you feel in the middle of making a picture?'" the American painter once said. "I can't answer. I think something takes over... you're lost in it."

Frankenthaler died in 2011 at the age of 83 after a career that spanned more than six decades. The engrossing power of her giant canvases helped change postwar American painting. Parks' photo was taken only a few years after Frankenthaler created *Mountains and Sea*, her 1952 breakthrough work. She painted it at age 23 after visiting Cape Breton Island, but the oil and charcoal canvas is more of an ephemeral impression of the Atlantic crashing against the rocks of Nova Scotia than a landscape per se. It reveals how she was influenced by abstract expressionists such as Jackson Pollock, but it also showcases her soak-stain technique of pouring diluted paint onto an unprimed canvas on the floor, allowing the watery oils to soak into the fabric and coalesce into amorphous fields of color.

The work was a "bridge from Pollock to what was possible," said fellow abstract painter Morris Louis, who, along with Frankenthaler, was among the originators of the Color Field movement, which emphasizes flat color planes removed from any figurative or subject matter, and includes artists such as Mark Rothko, Kenneth Noland, Sam Gilliam and Alma Thomas.

Frankenthaler was born in 1928, the daughter of a New York State Supreme Court judge, and grew up in comfortable surroundings. She studied art from an early age at the Dalton School, where she took lessons from the Mexican modernist painter Rufino Tamayo. At Bennington

1. According to her 2011 obituary in *The New York Times*, Frankenthaler experimented with color from a young age: At home, she would dribble nail polish into water and watch the color swirl and expand—an effect not dissimilar to the one she later achieved in her paintings.
—
—

2. Frankenthaler distanced herself from feminist readings of her work, but curators and critics have brought her into the conversation. For example, Judy Chicago's 1960s *Atmosphere* series—in which she set off colorful pyrotechnics in an attempt to "feminize the atmosphere"—bears visual similarities to Frankenthaler's work and has been exhibited alongside it.

> *"My safaris are all on the studio floor.*
> *That's where I take my danger."*

College in Vermont, she studied under Paul Feeley. After graduating in 1949, she returned to New York and her real education began through contact with other artists. "That shock, that recognition of what was going on in the art world in New York in those early '50s was tremendous for me and my painting," Frankenthaler told Charlie Rose in 1993, describing the effect of seeing Pollock's work on the floor of his studio. "The approach took painting literally off the easel, so instead of dealing head on with four sides and four corners, you felt the boundaries of the canvas, the scale of it, were endless. That thrust of shoulder as compared to wrist alone, and zeroing in and telescoping, was nothing compared to this sweep of handling the method and material in a different way."

Frankenthaler first exhibited in a group show in New York in 1950, and participated in the influential *9th Street* Art Exhibition of the following year. By the early 1960s, she was married to Robert Motherwell, an abstract expressionist of the New York School, and featuring in major international exhibitions as well as a retrospective of her own work. Over the following decades, as the Color Field movement expanded and changed, Frankenthaler's works spun like a phantasmagoric carousel, teasing representation with suggestive shapes and titles like *Milkwood Arcade* (1963), *Sphinx* (1976), *Cedar Hill* (1983), *Skywriting* (1996) and *Cloud Burst* (2002). She also experimented in mediums including paper, sculpture, printmaking, ceramics and tapestry while interest in her art grew.

By the time she died in Connecticut in 2011, Frankenthaler had taught at Harvard, Princeton and Yale, been the subject of numerous scholarly articles and books, and received many accolades including the National Medal of Arts. *Mountains and Sea* now hangs in the National Gallery of Art on extended loan.

In her private life, unlike in her art, Frankenthaler always drew within the lines. "My life," she told *The New York Times* in 1989, "is square and bourgeois. I like calm and continuity. I think as a person I'm very controlling, and I'm afraid of big risks. I'm not a skier or a mountain climber or a motorcyclist. And I'm not a safari girl—I never want to go

Right: Frankenthaler with paintings in progress in her New York studio in 1974 and, on the previous spread, a decade earlier in 1964. Because of her staining technique, and because she painted on unstretched canvas, many saw Frankenthaler's approach as haphazard. As she put it when talking about *Mountains and Sea*, it "looks to many people like a large paint rag, casually accidental and incomplete."

"There are no rules. That is how art is born, that is how breakthroughs happen."

on a safari. My safaris are all on the studio floor. That's where I take my danger." Perhaps as a result of her unabashedly square personality, she had her detractors: Some critics suggested her work, which shies from overt emotion and movement, was decorative and without depth. That's not too surprising given her comments like this one, also from *The New York Times* in 1989: "What concerns me when I work is not whether the picture is a landscape, or whether it's pastoral, or whether somebody will see a sunset in it. What concerns me is—did I make a beautiful picture?"

But anyone who sees a work like *Cool Summer* (1962) as merely beautiful is missing the point. This psychedelic color burst on a background of raw canvas is as much about the interplay of color, shape, gradation and empty space as what it might evoke in the viewer: a hazy memory, almost out of reach, of sunlight reflecting off water and scattering through trees on a summer day. Elizabeth Smith, executive director of the Helen Frankenthaler Foundation in New York, has a favorite Frankenthaler quote that sums up her aesthetic sensibility: "My pictures are full of climates, abstract climates and not nature per se, but a feeling. And the feeling of an order that is associated more with nature."

Frankenthaler broke new ground for female artists—including my own mother, Montreal painter Jennifer Hornyak—working in the decades after her. She's relevant to younger artists, too. "Frankenthaler's development of her own approach to abstraction, from her early introduction to Jackson Pollock's painting process coupled with her continual quest to expand the materials and means by which paintings are made,

are an inspiration to many of today's artists," says Smith. "We are also fortunate that a number of photographs exist of Frankenthaler in her studio; these and films showing Frankenthaler at work have inspired younger artists and informed them more deeply about her intensely physical painting process."

Just as her canvases grew denser, Frankenthaler's legacy has grown stronger. Renewed interest in the work of female painters has brought Frankenthaler into sharper focus in recent years, and a series of exhibitions from 2013, including shows at Gagosian Gallery and the Tate Modern, has further elevated Frankenthaler's stature. Her work is increasingly visible in museums: When Smith began her job in 2013, no New York museum had her works on view despite owning them. "Now, all the major museums here have put her work on view, sometimes multiple times," says Smith. "We've also seen this occur in other museums around the US ranging from LACMA and SFMOMA to the Walker Art Center and the Art Institute of Chicago, among many others, and in Europe in such museums as Museum Moderner Kunst Stiftung Ludwig (MUMOK) in Vienna."

Frankenthaler's greatest legacy, however, is surely her role as an iconoclast, an agent of change that moved art in new directions. She said it best in 1994: "There are no rules, that is one thing I say about every medium, every picture… that is how art is born, that is how breakthroughs happen. Go against the rules or ignore the rules, that is what invention is about."

Frankenthaler stands in front of *Sands* (in progress) in her studio in New York in 1964.

Frankenthaler in front of *One O'Clock* (in progress), and, to the left, *Red Boost* (also in progress), in her New York studio in 1966. Frankenthaler has become a popular muse, so much so that Proenza Schouler's 2015 fall collection was presented alongside two of her major prints. Designer Jack McCollough told *Vogue* that he was inspired by how she went into the studio "without any preconceived notions of what the final result was going to be. We really approached this season in the same way."

3. — 176

Nature

114 — 176

114
Rendered Impossible

120
Ron Finley

128
The Click Farm

136
Fresh Press

142
Jane Goodall

152
The Force of Nature

156
Rock Steady

166
Five Tips

Alexis Christodoulou is a self-taught 3D artist and designer based in Cape Town who creates imaginary architecture. *Kinfolk* commissioned Christodoulou for the series *Rendered Impossible* during the lockdown measures—and travel restrictions—brought on by COVID-19.

RON FINLEY:

MY GARDEN IS BASICALLY A BIG ASS *SOCIAL* EXPERIMENT.

In an excerpt from our forthcoming book, *The Kinfolk Garden*, *Stephanie d'Arc Taylor* meets *Ron Finley*. By sowing seeds in the barren public spaces of South Central Los Angeles, Finley reaped an unexpected reward: a new-found calling as a community activist. With each project that takes root, his motivation only grows. Photography by *Justin Chung*

This story is an exclusive excerpt from our forthcoming book, *The Kinfolk Garden*. Pre-order at Kinfolk.com now, or shop in stores worldwide from October 27.

Many who garden find their work restorative. Rarer are gardeners whose efforts have sparked political awakenings. Ron Finley grew up in the blighted South Central region of Los Angeles and went on to become a successful fashion designer and personal trainer.[1] But it was an act of gardening that crystallized his political consciousness.

In his 2012 ten-minute TED Talk (which has now surpassed 3.5 million views), Finley recounts the story of his political awakening in a series of pithy, and often delightfully unprintable, turns of phrase. South Central, he says, is what's known as a food desert—a term often used to describe inner-city areas where the only food options are fast-food chains and dollar stores. Disheartened by his community's limited access to fresh fruits and vegetables and the resulting sky-high rates of obesity, hypertension and other diet-related health problems, Finley transformed his parkway—West Coast terminology for the planted portion of a sidewalk—into a garden with vegetables and banana trees.[2]

As a result, the city of Los Angeles issued a citation, then a warrant for Finley's arrest, on the grounds that he was working public land without a permit. The public outcry that ensued successfully changed the law in Los Angeles that had prevented people from gardening on parkways. It also propelled Finley into a pioneering new career: community gardening activist.

"Gardening is the most therapeutic and defiant act you can do, especially in the inner city," Finley says on the phone from his new permanent project space in Los Angeles. "I've witnessed my garden become a tool for education, a tool for the transformation of my neighborhood."

Finley is adamant that home gardening has the opportunity to transform more than just his block in South LA. An increase in individuals' self-sufficiency can also positively disrupt the social and political systems that perpetuate self-defeating cycles in low-income communities.

"Just think about even one percent of us starting to grow our own food," Finley says. "Think how much money that would take out of the system, from healthcare to grocery stores. People growing their own food is dangerous [to the status quo]." Finley's number one tip to novice gardeners is indicative of his straight-talk approach: "Plant what you like to eat. Don't plant no shit you don't like."

But growing food to eat isn't Finley's only motivation to keep on mulching. "I'm not always planting for production. I also plant for beauty, for engagement. My garden is basically a big ass social experiment.[3] I'm an urban sociologist asking the question, 'How do people engage with something they're not used to seeing in the urban environment?'"

Finley's 'Russian Mammoth' sunflowers, in particular, have caused quite the stir in the neighborhood. The plants can stand ten feet tall, supporting flowers over a foot in diameter. "Kids stop and ask, 'Yo, is that real?' People have never seen anything like this. It's that kind of engagement I want."

NOTES

1. As a teenager, Finley took classes at a technical college in LA and made his own outfits. He soon started making clothes for friends, and the project eventually snowballed into a line—*Drop-dead Collexion*.

2. Finley's 70-by-40-foot produce garden came into its own during lockdown. In April, he told *The Guardian* that he had been living off produce and only left his property once (to buy fish) during the period of isolation.

3. Finley's most recent venture brings his message to a larger, albeit less diverse, audience: He now has a gardening series on the subscription-based MasterClass website, whose other experts include Serena Williams and Natalie Portman.

Much of Finley's garden is taken up with a large swimming pool that has long been given over to growing plants.

THE.

CLICK

Meet the influencers, and owners, fighting like cats and dogs for your likes. Words by Stephanie d'Arc Taylor
Photography by Gustav Almestål & Styling by Martin Persson

FARM.

Right: Barillo the alpaca wears a Burberry scarf. Left: Archie the duck frolics with a bottle of Bollinger. Previous: Snövit the cat towel-dries her hairless head, ready for another day in front of the camera.

"Part of the appeal of working with animals instead of humans is the absence of vitriol that has become a hallmark of social media."

A funeral procession winds through the fields outside of what's now Bonn, Germany. It's around 14,000 years ago. Life is solitary, poor, nasty, brutish and short. This being Germany, odds are it's cold as well. Among the departed is a 17-month-old puppy who died from a tooth infection. It will be accorded the same burial privileges as the two deceased humans also to be buried, and will rest with them in a common grave until being chanced upon by quarry workers in 1914. The so-called Bonn-Oberkassel dog was a harbinger of things to come. As the first undisputed example of a domesticated animal, it's the herald of a long, and sometimes sordid, saga of animal domestication and co-evolution that helped humans become the dominant species on the planet. Dogs helped us hunt, pigs and cattle improved our diets and cats flamboyantly eviscerated the rodents that soiled our food stores and spread disease.

But the care that went into the ancient puppy funeral in hardscrabble Stone Age Germany— where presumably people had a number of other pressing tasks— indicates that our pets also brought us companionship, comfort and joy.

This will not come as a surprise if you're one of the four million people who follow Doug the Pug on Instagram. Or the 1.8 million people who follow Mr. Pokee, the tribute account to a deceased hedgehog that now posts photos of a new hedgehog. Or the 2.9 million who follow the menagerie of foxes, chinchillas, opossums and reptiles at JuniperFoxx. Animals have always been a part of our story. Now they're in our Stories too. In a world where anxiety is rampant, and a stable future often far from assured, people are increasingly looking to our faunal friends for solace, both in person and on the internet. Frequently, pet ownership is taking the place of more traditional (some might say pre-digital) goals like starting a family or owning a home. As Jane Peh, co-founder of the Woof Agency, a marketing platform in Singapore, bluntly puts it: "Millennials want to have dogs and cats, nobody wants to have kids anymore."

Above: Bill Murray the dog shades himself from the glare of the spotlight with sunglasses by AliExpress. Galaxy the alpaca jumps on the Burberry scarf trend.

Marketing agencies have perked up their ears at the astonishing metrics of the most popular pet influencer accounts. Aside from the high follower counts, animal influencer accounts' engagement rates—a measure of how often followers like or comment on a post—are higher than average, says marketing specialist Nikita Baklanov. He works at the St. Petersburg office of HypeAuditor, an influencer marketing platform whose homepage chatbot is represented by a cat wearing sunglasses. Enterprising animal owners, and their corporate sponsors, have made fortunes. Take Tabatha Bundesen, an Arizona waitress whose brother posted a photo of her cat, Tardar Sauce, on Reddit in 2013. The next year, she disputed a tabloid report that her curmudgeonly pet—who the world knows as Grumpy Cat—had earned $100 million.

Whether or not it's true, Grumpy Cat became the official "spokescat" for Friskies, got her own Lifetime movie and was the subject of a book that made *The New York Times* bestseller list. In 2018, Bundesen won $710,000 in a copyright infringement case against a coffee company that made the Grumpy Cat Grumppuccino. Suffice it to say, she no

longer works as a waitress (despite Grumpy Cat's death in 2019).

But many of the humans behind pet influencer Instagram accounts do have other jobs, like Anna Mathias, who runs an Instagram page devoted to her hedgehogs, Lionel and Lilo. As of May 2020, the account has 146,000 followers. Mathias works full time handling the marketing for a bridalwear company in Charleston, South Carolina, and spends "at least an hour a day" on her hedgehogs' account. Her to-do list includes replying to followers' rhapsodic comments, performing critical social grooming by liking and following other Instagram accounts, producing photo shoots for her hedgehogs and working on campaigns with brands. Mathias has translated what seems like an innate knack for marketing into a lucrative side hustle. She adopted her first hedgehog in college from her sister's classmate after he announced that his new pet was "the worst." When she posted photos of Lionel on social media, he (and she) got attention. "Then I realized there's a whole world of animals on the internet," she says. "When you post animals, you get followers. There's a niche for literally everything."

The Instagram account grew naturally, accelerated by key shares of Lionel's photos by pop star Joe Jonas and Instagram itself. "It snowballed from there. After Instagram posted, we got 24,000 followers in 24 hours," Mathias says.

That's when the brands came knocking. To date, Mathias has partnered with the pet emporium Petco and this year's *Sonic the Hedgehog* movie based on the classic Japanese video game. There have been less obvious partnerships as well, including Away luggage, and furniture e-retailer Wayfair. "I do reach out when I see an obvious fit, but some companies reach out that I never would have thought of," she says. The details of each arrangement depend on a variety of factors, including the number of posts, exclusivity and free products. Mathias can make up to $6,000 per partnership. But that's just the tip of the iceberg: "Other people are making a lot more money," she says.

In Singapore, Jane Peh watched the rising stock of pet influencers

in her old job working with what she now calls, deadpan, "human influencers." "There were no agencies [in Asia] focused on pet profiles, so we decided to see if it would work," she says. A year later, they are working with more than 100 brands.

Peh says that for brands, part of the appeal of working with animals instead of humans is the absence of vitriol that has become a hallmark of social media. "With dogs, there's not much hate," she says. "How can you hate a dog?" Mathias echoes this: "It's a nice corner of the internet. The meanest thing someone said is that Lilo is chubby. I was like, 'can you not fat shame a hedgehog?'"

Another crucial factor for brands is that it would be nearly impossible for a hedgehog to be "canceled," Twitter parlance for having one's work and opinions invalidated and redacted wholesale from the cultural narrative. "If I were a brand working with, say, Logan Paul [the popular, controversy-prone YouTuber] I might be collateral damage," says Peh. "With pets, they're not going to get into a PR crisis. They're just going to eat, sleep and take photos."

But a popular animal Instagram account isn't just pets being adorable. Like human influencers, successful pages need an angle, whether it's posting a photo in response to every micro-trend à la Doug the Pug, or focusing on gorgeous photography, like Mr. Pokee. For Mathias, Lionel's page is simply about making people smile. "It's supposed to be a little thing that pops into your feed and brightens your day," she says. "It's just happy photos of hedgehogs."

The effect of happy pets on humans is more than easy prey for marketers, though. It's evidence of a calming connection that predates marketing, and even money. The bond between dogs and humans, writes Mark Derr in his book *How the Dog Became the Dog*, is evidence of convergent psychological evolution. It's a bond that invokes powerful emotions, he says, which "many today refer to as love—boundless, unquestioning love." In an age where many people get their emotional needs met on the internet, it seems natural for animals to be there too.

Top Left: Lisa de la Furr wears a Gucci scarf. Bottom Left: Lilly the hamster explores a pair of Gucci shoes. Right: Snövit spends her earnings on a bag by Loewe.

While in lockdown due to COVID-19, *Kinfolk* commissioned photographer Paul Rousteau and his partner, Marie Labarre, to produce the series *Fresh Press*.
All flowers were picked in the wild from the countryside surrounding the family's home in the south of France.

The backdrops were created outdoors, using drawings by Labarre and an ingenious way of using a scanner. "I use the scanner like a camera," says Rousteau. "I add color filters and drawings as the backgrounds to the flowers. Then, I open the scanner in the direction of the sun to produce glitches and flairs."

JA

From her perch in the tiny Tanzanian nature reserve of Gombe, primatologist *Jane Goodall* changed how we understand the nature of chimpanzees—and ourselves. Words by *Katie Calautti*

NE

NATURE

"People go, 'You need to slow down.' But I have to go quicker."

Jane Goodall knew she loved apes long before she penned her first field notes in the Tanzanian wilds of Gombe. When the pioneering primatologist was one year old, her father gifted her a stuffed chimpanzee named Jubilee. The now-hairless love-worn toy remains one of her prized possessions. As a child, Goodall managed a coterie of creatures at her family home in Bournemouth, England—starting with handfuls of earthworms and sea snails that she snuck into bed and progressing to her first field research project, a stakeout in a henhouse, at the age of five.

"When I was a little girl, I used to dream as a man, because I wanted to do things that women didn't do back then such as traveling to Africa, living with wild animals," Goodall wrote in a 2018 *Time* article. "I didn't have any female ex-plorers or scientists to look up to but I was inspired by Dr. Dolittle, Tarzan, and Mowgli in *The Jungle Book*."

In 1957, while visiting a friend in Kenya, Goodall met famed paleoanthropologist Louis Leakey. Leakey hired her as his secretary and later brought her on an archeological dig at Olduvai Gorge in Tanzania, where he noticed Goodall's patience, independence and keen observation skills. He'd long wanted to conduct a field study of chimpanzees, who share 98.6% of the same DNA as humans. At the time, next to nothing was known about chimps in the wild.

Leakey procured funding, and offered Goodall the job, even though she didn't have a college degree.[1] "Louis didn't care about academic credentials," Goodall recounted in her book *Reason for Hope*. "He told me he preferred that his chosen researcher should go into the field with a mind unbiased by scientific theory."

On July 14, 1960, 26-year-old Goodall arrived at the Gombe Stream National Park on the eastern shores of Lake Tanganyika in Tanzania. Her only companions were her mother, Vanne, and a local cook named Dominic. They lived on a shoestring budget, working out of an old Army tent and bathing in streams.

"I knew perfectly well that if results didn't come through, Louis wouldn't be able to raise further money," Goodall wrote in *Reason for Hope*. "I was terrified of letting him down." After two frustrating months, she was accepted into the fold by a chimp she named David Greybeard, and soon she was assigning names and personalities to every primate community member.

Goodall's discovery in 1960 that chimpanzees make and use tools is considered one of the greatest achievements of 20th-century animal scholarship, and her field research at Gombe, in which she immersed herself in their habitat, redefined the relationship between humans and animals.

Goodall's history-making observation came when she caught David poking blades of grass into a termite mound to scoop out and eat the bugs, and later saw chimpanzees stripping leaves off of twigs to fish for termites. The chimps weren't just employing tools, they were also demonstrating modification—behaviors thought to be unique to humans. Leakey famously proclaimed of her discovery, "Now we must redefine 'tool,' redefine 'man,' or accept chimpanzees as humans."

The iconic field images of Goodall clad in khaki shorts and T-shirt, bag slung over her shoulder, binoculars in hand, blonde hair in a signature low ponytail, scaling steep slopes and trees alike—sometimes barefoot—with a determined, watchful expression fixed on her face are as much a part of the public consciousness today as they were 60 years ago.

Goodall herself has remained nonplussed by the attention. "There's this glamorous young girl out in the jungle with potentially dangerous animals," Goodall told *National Geographic* in 2017. "People like romanticizing and people were looking at me as though I was that myth that they had created in their mind. Articles at the time touted Goodall's "fragile" and "uncommonly pretty" appearance, branding her "a comely miss." In a 1963 wire story, Goodall's comment, "I'm becoming more arboreal" segued to, "Miss Goodall appears more ethereal than arboreal. The slender blonde English girl looks as if she should be serving tea to the village vicar, not tracking chimpanzees in Africa."

"The media produced some rather sensational articles, emphasizing my blonde hair and referring to my legs," Goodall wrote in the 2018 *Time* article. "Some

scientists discredited my observations because of this—but that did not bother me so long as I got the funding to return to Gombe and continue my work... If my legs helped me get publicity for the chimps, that was useful."

In 1962 Goodall became one of the few people in the University of Cambridge's history to be admitted to work for a Ph.D. without a B.A. "I was quickly told that I had done my study all wrong," Goodall told *Time*. "I should have numbered the chimps rather than given them names, and I could not talk about their personalities, minds, or emotions, as those features were unique to humans."

Goodall stood her ground with professors and rejected what she perceived as coldness in their approach. "You can make observations that are absolutely scientifically accurate even while having empathy for the being you are studying," she wrote. This approach is part of what's made Goodall the world's foremost expert on chimpanzees. "It was clear they had emotions like happiness, sadness, fear," she told *The New York Times* in 2019. "That they had a dark and brutal side, but also love, compassion, altruism."

Goodall's initial stay at Gombe was extended through a grant from *National Geographic*, and she was joined by Dutch wildlife photographer Hugo van Lawick. Their collaboration on the 1965 National Geographic Society film *Miss Goodall and the Wild Chimpanzees*, which was viewed by an estimated 25 million North Americans (a massive amount, even by today's standards), made Goodall a star. The two married in 1964 and had a son, Hugo Eric Louis—known affectionately as Grub—in 1967. They divorced 10 years later after Goodall's work kept her in Gombe and van Lawick's

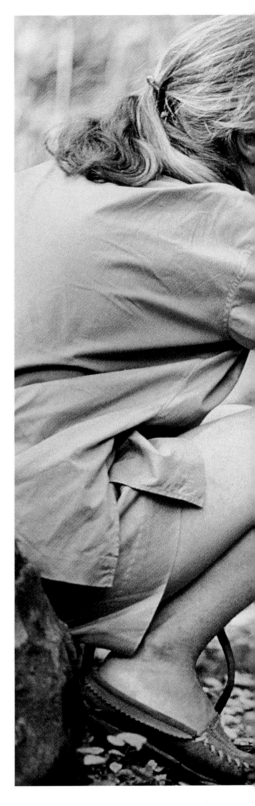

Goodall's research has shed light on chimpanzees, humankind's closest living relatives, for more than 60 years. Her work has redefined species conservation to include the needs of local people and the environment—a subject which she now travels the world to lecture on.

"*People were looking at me as though I was that myth that they had created in their mind.*"

Left Photograph: CBS via Getty Images. Previous Spread: National Geographic Studios / AF archive / Alamy Stock Photo

---

NOTE

1. Along with Goodall, Leakey also encouraged occupational therapist Dian Fossey to study mountain gorillas in Rwanda and student Birutė Galdikas to study orangutans in Borneo. The three women became known as the Trimates and went on to become prominent scientists and important scholars in the field of primatology. Today, Galdikas continues her field research into orangutans—among the lengthiest continuous studies of a mammal ever conducted—and campaigns on behalf of primate conservation and the preservation of rainforest environments. Fossey published *Gorillas in the Mist*, a seminal account of her studies at Karisoke Research Center, two years before she was murdered in her cabin at a remote camp in Rwanda in December 1985. It has been theorized that her murder was linked to her conservation efforts. Serious threats to the survival of mountain gorillas persist, from irresponsible development to climate change—and now COVID-19. Mountain gorillas share about 98% of human DNA and can catch respiratory diseases from people. Scientists warned in April 2020 that COVID-19 poses an "existential threat" to primates and that, for mountain gorillas, the introduction of a new, highly infectious disease could be a "potential extinction-level event."

Essay:

The Force of Nature

Words by Ana Kinsella

From microwaveable meals to makeup, skin creams to sink cleaner, "laboratory formulated" products used to fly off the shelves. Now, Mother Nature sells more than science; consumers want everything raw, clean and organic. What prompted the shift and what, if anything, do we risk losing when "natural" becomes a synonym for "good"? Ana Kinsella investigates.

Humans have a funny way of imposing a moral code on just about anything. Imagine, for a moment, explaining to an extraterrestrial that one plate of food (an organic green salad) is apparently virtuous and wholesome, while another plate (a pile of golden, salty fries) is more delicious, but bears a kind of guilt. Both foods provide sustenance. Surely, the extraterrestrial might suggest, that should be enough for us humans. Guilt or virtue, you would then need to explain, are social constructs that we have become quite attached to.

There's a kind of virtue ascribed to choosing "natural." Organic foods, we believe, are better than processed ones. Following a paleo diet indicates that you care about your health and your body and are willing to do what it takes to cherish it—just like our cave-dwelling ancestors. Experiencing natural childbirth is a badge of honor among many mothers, as though requiring medical intervention is cheating. Lately, the extreme of this idea has emerged in anti-vaccine sentiment, where parents risk the lives of their children—and others—by refusing vaccinations, often on the grounds that inoculations themselves are unnatural in some way.

The conflict between science and the appeal of the "natural" is centuries old. *Natural*, a new book by Alan Levinovitz, professor of religion at James Madison University, puts forward the idea that religion underpins the notion that natural is best. Levinovitz believes that "natural" is a secular synonym for "holy." What is unnatural can only be the work of man. He cites, for example, the suspicious reaction to the Impossible Burger, the meat-like plant-based burger launched in 2016.[1] That same year, the US Food and Drug Administration invited comments from consumers on the meaning of "natural food." Many mentioned theology as a basis for choosing meat. "Natural," reads one, "should be limited to those ingredients that have been created by God."

Religious or otherwise, food is often the site of much cultural and emotional anxiety. "You're being good," one colleague might say to another who has passed over the appealing supermarket meal deal for a brown-bag lunch. But a homemade meal in and of itself doesn't have an inherent moral superiority. The moral dimension of the natural is something that we superimpose on it.

Today, "natural" is a marketing term, and one that is muddy at best. Data cited in Levinovitz's *Natural* claims that more than half of Americans say they prefer "all natural" foods. Food historian and author Annie Gray points out the danger in the word's instability. "The term is never well-defined," she tells me. "And that, of course, is very useful in the cynical world of marketing." But what is it that consumers are looking for when they seek out natural food?

In recent years, the turn to the natural has been accelerated by instances in which the alternative has proved itself to be less appealing. Jonathan

1. Blurring the line between what might be considered vice and virtue cuisine, Burger King announced the introduction of The Impossible Whopper in 2019 —a version of its Whopper sandwich filled with a vegetarian patty from Impossible Foods.

—

2. Goop writes of its belief that "whole food is the cornerstone of health," and describes many of its recipes as "relatively virtuous and free of common allergens." Paltrow's cookbook, *The Clean Plate: Eat, Reset, Heal*, features over 100 recipes using what she describes as "clean ingredients."

Safran Foer's 2009 book, *Eating Animals*, investigated the reality of industrialized farming, while the UK and Ireland's horsemeat scandal in 2013 revealed the dangerous lack of transparency in the food chain. But there's a risk, Gray says, of throwing the baby out with the bathwater when we prize all things natural in our food choices. "The food chain is highly complex. Do all consumers understand the regulations around organic, and that it is an entirely constructed definition? I doubt it."

That complexity doesn't prevent the interweaving of natural lifestyle choices and the moral high ground, though. For modern consumers, choosing supposedly natural goods over processed options signals something. *I'm using coconut oil instead of chemicals to remove my makeup,* the fresh-faced celebrity might tell us in a magazine interview. In doing so, she rises above the rest of us—the poor, ignorant and lazy who pour hazardous chemicals directly on our skin. Gwyneth Paltrow's Goop is a commercial empire built on the perception of natural consumer choices as a kind of luxury reserved for the beautiful and well-off.[2] Levinovitz notes that the shift from "natural" to "morally superior" is a slippery slope, and one that brings class and privilege into its remit. "It's no coincidence that natural foods and products are very expensive, and 'natural' child-rearing requires time that many people just don't have," he explains. "This turns 'naturalness' into a form of classism, where the impure, unnatural lower classes cannot compete in spiritual cleanliness with the upper classes. There's nothing wrong with valuing natural products because you like them, but don't confuse 'natural' with 'better' or 'holy.'"

There are obvious benefits that come with investigating our health and agricultural practices. The rhetoric around natural beauty has helped dangerous activities like the use of sunbeds fall out of favor among the young, for example. And heightened scrutiny of the chemicals in our cosmetics and food is a good thing. But we may also risk losing something when we automatically favor that which seems to be natural.

"There's nothing wrong with valuing natural products because you like them, but don't confuse 'natural' with 'better' or 'holy.'"

In agriculture, science has made farms more efficient, and technological advances in recent years have helped farmers to work with the environment to have less of an impact. Organic farming, Gray says, is never going to feed the world on its own. "Farmers markets are delightful, but they cost more. We need an informed discussion around food and foodways which is not largely held around the kitchen islands of the well-off, I'm afraid. And we should certainly not be equating 'science' with 'bad'… or even 'processed' with 'bad'—there are a lot of degrees of processing, and it's possible to buy natural vegan food which is so highly processed that I, at least, would balk at buying it."

Levinovitz says that when he first approached the topic of nature, he thought that it, too, was a social construct. "But there must be an important difference between Yellowstone National Park and New York City," he observes. "If there's no such thing as nature, then what exactly are we trying to conserve? If wilderness is a construct, why not install rides in national parks?" The fuzzy point at which our moral values intersect with our concept of nature is where the problem arises. "But the truth is that it doesn't matter whether something is unnatural or not." What matters, he continues, is "whether it causes joy or brings suffering."

Science, after all, has managed to alleviate so much suffering. Antibiotics, by any standard, could be considered unnatural, but they enable us to live longer and healthier lives. And when the world is facing a crisis, it is to science that we look for a route to safety. Nature doesn't have to be at odds with that; it's possible, in fact, for science and nature to work together as two distinct forces. There's an opportunity to prove this right in front of us: Climate breakdown poses an existential threat to life on Earth as we know it. If there is a workable and just solution, it'll be developed in laboratories as much as in the natural environment. "In the future, the solutions to our problems will be a diverse combination of 'natural' and 'unnatural' approaches," Levinovitz concludes. "That's not something to feel guilty or conflicted about."

ROCK STEADY

A breath of fresh air amid the ancient Stone Forest of southwestern China. Photography by Jumbo Tsui @ Styling by Evan Feng

Models: Pan Haowen & Huang Shixin. Makeup & Hair: Daniel Zhang.

Above: Pan wears a shirt and tie by Gucci and a skirt by Ferragamo. Left and Previous: Pan wears a sleeveless jacket and skirt by AMI.
Huang wears a suit by AMI and a T-shirt by Brunello Cucinelli.

Above: Huang wears a suit by Givenchy and a shirt by Prada. Left: Pan wears a dress by Amiri.

Pan wears a pink poplin dress by Valentino and a black silk dress by Maison Sans Titre.

Above: Pan wears a jacket by Blue Erdos, shirt by Tommy Zhong and a skirt by Brunello Cucinelli. Left: Huang wears a trench coat by Acne Studios.

Five tips for appreciating and understanding the wilder corners of the natural world. Photography by Gustav Almestål & Set Design and Styling by Andreas Frienholt

TIPS

Bug Out

I ate an ant and I liked it. Apologies, Katy Perry, but this is important. I tried ants because, according to the UN Food and Agriculture Organization, livestock production takes up nearly one-third of the Earth's entire landmass. And the animals themselves generate nearly 20% of the world's greenhouse emissions. That's more than all the cars, trains, boats and planes put together. In the search for a sustainable protein, it's sink or swim time. Fortunately, 2 billion of our planet's 8 billion inhabitants indulge in a wondrously diverse protein source. Predominantly in Africa and Asia, people eat more than 1,900 edible insect species as part of their normal diet. The most common nibble is beetles, followed by caterpillars in second place, with hymenoptera (bees, ants and wasps) in third. And don't worry, there's always a seasonal item on the bug menu. In Thailand, for example, that means tortoise beetles (bitterly crunchy) in January, damselflies (with hints of crab) in July and mole crickets (a smoky umami tang) around Christmastime.

So what's the issue? The Western world has an "ick factor" when it comes to eating bugs, although this doesn't stop them from caging intelligent mammals for food consumption. Fortunately, peer attitudes can quickly change. Commentators cite the example of lobsters, an invertebrate arthropod like caterpillars or cicadas. These giant sea insects were once deemed so foul that American jailers were prohibited from feeding lobster to prisoners more than a few times per week as they were considered a "cruel and unusual" punishment food. Now edible insects are becoming aspirational. Pioneer foodies can show off their eco-credentials by purchasing chili 'n' lime crunchy crickets from mainstream food stores. Alternatively, insects can be pressed into a paste then mixed into protein bars or shakes.

And while cows fart 200 liters of methane into the atmosphere per day, insects are integral to the wider food chain as plant pollinators. (Still, nothing is perfect: In Europe and the US, mealworms—like cows—are reared for consumption in factory conditions. Cue energy requirements, food miles and moral hand-wringing.) Achieved thoughtfully, a more insect-centric diet might prove tasty, nutritious and environmentally beneficial. Now that's holier than cow. Grubs up!

Get Muddy

Lara Maiklem has spent over 15 years on the banks of the River Thames in London, kneeling in the mud on the foreshore and staring for hours at a time at the same small patch of land. Maiklem is a mudlark: She looks for old objects —pins, buttons, clay pipe stems— that have been discarded in the river by long-forgotten ordinary Londoners. Unlike most rivers that run through cities, the Thames' tidal rise and fall mean it's constantly turning up new treasures. Maiklem's *Sunday Times* bestselling book about her hobby, *Mudlarking* (*Mudlark* in the US), is a hybrid of history, memoir and nature writing.

BG: *What drew you to mudlarking?* **LM:** I grew up on a farm and spent an awful lot of time on my own, wandering across fields and playing in the hedgerows. It taught me to enjoy my own company: If you don't, you can become strangely lonely. When I came to London, I looked for peace and solitude and discovered the river. I used to go almost every day. Now that I've moved out, I go every weekend.

BG: *You've spent so much time with the river over the years—what have you noticed?* **LM:** It brings nature into the city. The weather is different there: With no buildings to shelter you, the wind is raw, the rain falls on you properly. In the city, all you can smell is fried food and pollution, but when you are face to face with the river, you smell it. It's different across the seasons: often a silty, slightly rotten, woody smell that gets into your hands and clothes—you end up carrying it home on the train. In summer, it smells hot, pungent, of algae. When storms are coming, it's almost dry, chalky. You get a hard stone smell in the winter.

BG: *How have your finds changed?* **LM:** Up until the early 1900s, people took from nature to make their things, and when they lost them or threw them away, they gave them back to nature, and nature broke them down. When plastic became commonly used, we stopped working with nature and started working against it. What I find varies with seasons: tennis balls during Wimbledon, old Christmas trees in the new year. After the coronavirus, I can guarantee we'll find disposable gloves and masks.

BG: *What about the river's health?* **LM:** Since 1957, when the river was declared "biologically dead," they've cleaned it up. There are around 125 species of fish; oysters are making a comeback in the estuary. I found a colony of seahorses on the Isle of Dogs, and saw a seal by the Oxo Tower. Having said that, there's still raw sewage, and the rubbish floats a few inches below the surface, so you don't see most of it. I was at Hammersmith, and the foreshore felt strangely spongy. I looked down and found I was standing on an island made entirely from wet wipes. There was a poor duck trying to make a nest on it. Even if wet wipes say they are flushable, they're not! They're changing the river's geography: They catch on the bends. Once the super sewer that's currently under construction starts working, the river will be cleaner than it has been for hundreds of years.

BG: *What do you get from mudlarking?* **LM:** As soon as I get down to the foreshore, I leave everything behind, and I can just let my mind wander. It's great therapy. I come away from the river with my shoulders down: a different, much nicer person.

Navigate Nature

Trees don't grow as children draw them—straight trunked, bushy leaves at the top, maybe a couple of branches off in either direction. Instead, they grow with the sun. In the Northern Hemisphere, when the sun is at its highest point, giving out most of its energy, it is due south. Trees here will naturally be thicker and greener on their southern side. If you are ever lost, look for a tree, and you'll have a ready-made compass point.

Go closer and you'll find more clues. While on one side branches grow straight out toward the sun, branches on the opposite side will reach upward, trying to peer over and catch the light. Leaves on either side are different, too. Sun leaves are thicker, paler. Shade leaves are larger, thinner, darker. Then, look for the insects: Trees tend to bend with the prevailing wind, and spiders will spin their webs to shelter from that wind. If you know where south is, you can gauge from which direction the wind is blowing by looking for a spiderweb. As well as telling you where you are, nature can tell you what you're near. Certain butterflies only inhabit areas near woodland. Dragonflies fly near water. Stinging nettles grow in phosphate-rich soil—the kind of soil that comes from agriculture. If you're lost in the wilderness, they are a clue that civilization is near at hand.

Weather can do the same. If you're near the English or Scottish coast in the summer, when warm air passes over the North Sea, you'll likely feel your face speckled with a cold fog called *haar*, also rather beautifully known as *sea fret*, that moves quickly inland. Walk toward it and you'll find the coast soon enough. Bodies of water—coastlines or rivers—are also good for the navigation technique known as "handrailing," the practice of choosing a linear feature to follow alongside.

The word "disoriented" comes from French, meaning to turn from the east. Turn away from the sun and you will become lost, confused, bewildered. It seems apt we have kept hold of the word because contained within it is a solution: Look to nature, and you will soon find out where you are.

Home Grown

For accidental houseplant killers and New Yorkers with rentals in need of cheer, Lisa Muñoz is here to help. In her unusual line of work as a plant stylist, she hand-picks houseplants and ceramic pots for clients, and styles them in homes and offices across the city. Her company, Leaf and June, will even drop by for weekly watering.

SMS: *Where does your love of plants come from?* **LM:** My grandparents had pretty extensive gardens in San Antonio, where there are desert plants everywhere and cacti in parking lots. But they had papayas in their backyard, which I think is so weird for Texas. They grew peppers, melons, tomatoes, chiles and calamansi—these citrus fruits you find in the Philippines, where they're from. In college I got a Home Depot plant. That's everyone's first foray! I loved seeing plants grow and started taking classes at the Brooklyn Botanic Garden. A friend said, "You're really good at this, you should make it your job." I was like "That's not a thing. People don't do that."

SMS: *You ended up proving yourself wrong! Where do you shop for plants now?* **LM:** I work with growers on Long Island. It's very different from the New York flower market—they have these beautiful greenhouses and oftentimes something will stop me in my tracks. When *Pilea peperomioides* [Chinese money plant] was making a comeback and were hard to come by, New Yorkers were paying $40 to $60 for tiny plants. So they propagated some and suddenly had greenhouses full of affordable baby plants.

SMS: *What are some of the common problems that people have with houseplants?* **LM:** Overwatering. Less is more. But overwatering is easy to solve, and it shows that people want to devote time to their plants.

SMS: *Are you an advocate of talking to plants?* **LM:** It can't hurt. It's interesting to see how rapidly they decline if they're left alone. In our old apartment we had an office we didn't use, but [because] it had the best light we kept the plants there. And so many of them died, just because we weren't in there with them.

SMS: *How can houseplants make a difference in peoples' everyday lives?* **LM:** Clients from years ago still email me with a picture of a plant that's tripled in size—it's therapeutic for people to take care of them. Just like it feels good to care for people or pets. Maybe living in a forest with beautiful trees outside is the only time when not having houseplants is fine. Tending to them is so rewarding; even though lugging a big plant into the shower is kind of a pain in the ass, I'm like, "I'm glad I did that."

SMS: *Which varieties do you have a soft spot for?* **LM:** I love plants that trail beautifully, like satin pothos. Mine is six feet, cut from a plant I gave to a client when they wanted something long and mature. It broke my heart!

SMS: *Where do you look for ideas?* **LM:** For me, it's about finding plants that you wouldn't necessarily see everywhere. But I'm also not opposed to putting something simple like a snake plant—the kind you might see in a bank—into a home. The [choice of] planter makes it into a unique thing that doesn't feel sterile or overused.

SMS: *I like the idea of seeing those overlooked plants in a new light.* **LM:** Exactly. I used to hate snake plants until I figured out that seeing them at home is totally different from like, vacant vestibules.

Imagine settling in for a cozy night in front of the television screen. You're in the mood for something light, so you slap on *Project Runway*, or maybe an old reality show like *The Hills* if you're feeling nostalgic. Are you scandalized to learn that these shows are heavily edited, or even scripted? Would you prefer to watch things happen as they really might have—Lauren Conrad and co. acting like co-workers instead of archnemeses—or do you get a kick out of the dramatized catfights and mascara-smudging tears?

Similar questions have come up with nature documentaries. In 2011, it was revealed that the venerated BBC series *Frozen Planet* had filmed its footage of newborn polar bear cubs in a zoo. Is this footage misleading? Yes, since it's presented in the context of wild polar bears lumbering hungrily across the frozen tundra. Does it spoil the fun? Probably not. It took the BBC's various teams four years with hands frozen to telephoto cameras in the Arctic to gather the footage used in 2019's *Our Planet* series. Given that most of us have elected to pursue indoor careers, an hour of highlights from the days of Arctic mammal's lives, arranged into gently dramatic story lines, complemented by staccato strings and grandfatherly narration is as natural as we want to get on a Tuesday night.

Other tricks can be sneakier for viewers, and more harmful to animals and habitats. In 1958, producers of the Disney program *White Wilderness* purchased hundreds of lemmings from some Canadian kids and forced them to jump off a cliff, thus "proving" that lemmings commit mass suicide to control their own population. More recently, filmmakers have copped to putting M&M's inside a roadkill carcass to get a bear-sniffing money shot. "Film costs $125 a roll," one nature documentary host protested in 1996, after a similar scandal. "We don't have 100 hours of film to leave rolling until one of these fish grabs a bug."

Watching nature documentaries might feel more sophisticated than watching *The Hills*, especially in the last two minutes of each episode when David Attenborough starts talking about global warming. All told, they are probably more edifying than much else on television, and we can always hope that they will inspire younger generations to treat the Earth better than their parents did. But perhaps nature—real nature—is sometimes better left alone, or even faked in a studio. Those polar bear cubs and their exhausted mother don't need to be disturbed.

Watch and Learn

On the unnatural narratives of nature shows.
Words by *Stephanie d'Arc Taylor*

4.

Directory

178 — 192

178
Peer Review

179
Object Matters

180
Cult Rooms

182
Bad Idea

183
Last Night

184
Anne Tyler

186
Crossword

187
Correction

Peer Review

Michelle Dean, author of *Sharp: The Women Who Made an Art of Having an Opinion* celebrates *Renata Adler.*

The first time I remember encountering Renata Adler, she was mid-skirmish in the pages of *Harper's Magazine*. It was the year 2000. She had just published a book called *Gone: The Last Days of the New Yorker* and apparently everyone in New York was angry with her. *The New York Times*, she reported, had published no fewer than eight pieces rebutting the book. She wrote of it as "institutional carpet bombing." Never one to shy from drama, I was intrigued.

That said, for a person like me, from the provinces (read: Canada), much of the piece was impenetrable. I didn't live among people who tracked bylines, let alone mastheads. No one I knew had opinions about which regime at *The New Yorker* was best. The idea that a magazine could so closely resemble a soap opera, or perhaps a Roman epic—fiefdoms and rivalries and hard-set preferences for umlauts that would shape generations of readers and writers—still counted as a revelation.

Adler was so blunt and funny that I went out and bought a copy of *Gone* at my Montreal bookstore. Which marked the first but not the last time I'd get lost in untangling the institutional history of the literati. In New York, of course, Ad-

ler's gadfly ways were known long before *Gone* was published. Born in 1937 to a Jewish couple who had fled Nazi Germany, she began working at *The New Yorker* in 1962. Before she was 30, she was taking aim at Norman Podhoretz and any number of other fatuous figures that the hothouse of New York media and publishing produced. In the late '60s she briefly moved over to *The New York Times* to write some of the most blistering film reviews of all time. Her first began, "Even if your idea of a good time is to watch a lot of middle-aged Germans, some of them very fat, all reddening, grimacing, perspiring, and falling over Elke Sommer, I think you ought to skip *The Wicked Dreams of Paula Schultz*."

After a year, Adler returned to *The New Yorker* where she remained until the early 1990s. She'd eventually attack the magazine's own film critic, Pauline Kael, at length, go to law school, and write a number of simultaneously infuriating and brilliant pieces about law and culture. You'll have to read *Gone* to find out why she ended up leaving *The New Yorker* again, though the book is out of print and difficult to find. But the search will be worth it.

NOTE

Late in a critical career where she'd never been known to pull punches, Adler began writing fiction. Her first novel, *Speedboat*, was both formally challenging—it is a novel-in-anecdotes, paragraphs describing discrete events with the reader left to divine the link between them. The story, such as it is, chronicles the life of Jen Fain, a young journalist, in 1970s New York. Jen is just as simultaneously disillusioned and brilliant as the writer who created her, a woman more prone to observing the absurdities of her life than to living fully in the moment. And for that reason, *Speedboat* can be riotously funny. A boyfriend, for example, is described as a "Calvinist in reverse; that is, he was uncompromisingly bohemian."

Left Photograph: Sebastian Kim / August Image. Right Photograph: *Speedboat* by Renata Adler. Published by New York Review Books.

A potted history of the bonsai tree.

Photograph: Gustav Almestål. Styling: Andreas Frienholt

KATIE CALAUTTI

Object Matters

The impulse to bring the outside in is centuries old, a fact that bonsai trees are testament to. Beginning in the first century A.D., the Chinese practice of *penjing*, "pot scenery," replicated the natural world in realistic miniature. Enthusiasts believed that scaling down landscapes gave them access to nature's powers, which they felt became more potent in the process.

The horticultural technique of raising trees in small landscapes was first only indulged in by the elite using natively collected specimens. Ancient images from around 700 A.D. show the tiny universes being given as gifts. According to artistic depictions, the practice was adopted by the Japanese around the beginning of the 14th century. But the Japanese style focused only on trees instead of on full landscapes. In fact, "bonsai," the Japanese word for the craft, means "a tree planted in a shallow container," reinforcing how the art form hinges largely upon the symbiotic relationship between plant and tray.

Gardeners train bonsai trees into diminutive natural shapes through a combination of planting in small containers, pinching buds, wiring branches and restrictive root and branch pruning—most bonsai trees are under four feet. Bonsai plants can be made from any tree species, and because they're cultivated from full-sized tree seeds, they can grow full-sized fruit. Their value is inherent in their need for meticulous care—most bonsai trees must be maintained daily.

By the late 18th century, bonsai was enjoyed by people of all social classes in Asia. And the practice had evolved from a mythical, esoteric approach to one of hobbyists focusing on design. As travel to the East and migration to the West increased in the late 19th century, the bonsai practice spread.

Since World War II, Western influence has altered the types of trees cultivated and the plants' aesthetic shapes. The release of the *Karate Kid* movies in the 1980s spurred a younger generation to take up bonsai, and now plants are mass-produced in over a dozen styles. But however they come to fruition, bonsai trees may just outlast us all—one of the longest-living bonsai trees, a ficus, is estimated to be 1,000 years old.

Cult Rooms

On a barren stretch of British coastline, *Derek Jarman's* Prospect Cottage is a bold celebration of beauty against all odds.

"For our house is our corner of the world. It is our first universe, a real cosmos in every sense," wrote Gaston Bachelard in *The Poetics of Space.* Prospect Cottage in Dungeness was the cosmos of Derek Jarman, the visionary British filmmaker, writer and artist. It is a strange building in an even stranger setting. Dungeness is a 12-square-mile stretch of shingle and marsh on the Kent coast. It is typically described as post-apocalyptic, despite being one of Britain's richest nature reserves thanks to the lichens, insects and migratory birds who temporarily call it home. This belies its appearance as a barren wasteland, punctuated by a line of squat wooden buildings, loomed over by two nuclear power stations. All around the headland the sea glisters or roars, depending on the weather.

Crouched in the shingle like a wounded blackbird a hundred yards or so from the sea's edge is Prospect Cottage. Black-tarred with bright yellow window frames on the outside, clad with pine tongue-and-groove on the inside, the four-room Victorian fisherman's cottage would today be called a seaside bolt-hole or, worse, a cabin. Jarman moved here before we started fetishizing small spaces and became self-conscious about re-embracing nature. For him it was a challenge as much as a sanctuary. His life at Prospect Cottage is memorialized in the diaries he kept from 1989 to 1990, published in 1991 as *Modern Nature.* "It was a stake in the future, and it also led him deep into remembrance of the past," writes Olivia Laing in her introduction to the 2018 reissue of the book. Both house and garden provided therapy, distraction, focus, clarity and endless activity.

Jarman was diagnosed as HIV-positive in December 1986. Thereafter, he spent an increasing amount of time at Prospect Cottage, which he had bought earlier that year on a whim following his father's death. *Modern Nature* reveals his daily tussle with the mundane and the dramatic, with life and death, the past and the present, and more literally between man and nature—his fight to grow a garden in the weather-blasted shingle around "Prospect," as he referred to his cottage.

Yet Jarman was definitely not a tragic figure and Prospect Cottage was not somewhere he retreated to in preparation for death. It was a place of great joy, a source of inspiration and productivity. It was a celebration of life. From furniture to gardening to writing to painting, Jarman created tirelessly. In 1990 he shot his masterpiece, *The Garden,* here. "First and foremost the cottage was always a living thing—a practical toolbox for his work," his friend and protégé Tilda Swinton said to the crowd at an Artfund fundraiser to save Prospect Cottage and its garden in January 2020. The bid was successful and both house and garden have a secure future with a public program and residencies for artists, academics, writers, gardeners and filmmakers.

Jarman poured himself into Prospect Cottage and his garden. The house is filled with hagstone necklaces, religious icons and paintings by himself and his friends, assemblages of found objects and tools for writing, painting, gardening and household improvements. It is impossible to separate the garden from the cottage. Both are windows into Jarman's soul, expressions of his imagination, his vision and tenacity. It is often written that a garden exists as a triumph of life in the face of death. The image of Jarman in his coveralls, wheeling a barrow of flotsam along the shingle to construct totems of iron, shell, stone and bone among the poppies is the embodiment of endurance. "I waited a lifetime to build my garden, and built my garden with the colours of healing on the sepia shingles of Dungeness," Jarman wrote. "Here was a garden to soothe the mind. For my garden was a place of rest for weary feet, and my tired eyes."

In his diaries, Jarman wrote of how his garden provided him with comfort amid the AIDS crisis. Photograph: Geraint Lewis

ALEX ANDERSON

Bad Idea: Lawns

A green and pleasant death knell for diversity.

Here's the plan: Foster immaturity, discourage diversity, squander resources. Or, put another way: Mow your grass often to keep it from flowering or putting down deep roots; poison or pull any plants that aren't grass (call these weeds); and use lots of fresh water, nutrients and energy to keep the sward artificially verdant and trim. The result, the ubiquitous turf lawn—that sink of weekend time, that field of neighborly conformity and not-so-neighborly competition—may look green and nice, but it is a surprisingly bad idea.

Although livestock in northern countries have chewed and trampled grassy fields to closely shorn uniformity for as long as people can recall, ornamental lawns have only been around for a few hundred years. These green carpets devised for French and English gardens offered bold testament to aristocratic hubris—demonstrating the will and resources to make productive agricultural land not merely useless but costly. Before Edwin Budding devised a machine to mow lawns in 1830, laborers had to scythe and shear grass to keep it looking neat from chateau windows. Such tidiness and uniformity were sure signs of gentility.

The modest bluegrass and fescue lawns we've inherited still seem to offer a sense of civility. Recent research bears this out, showing that urban residents associate well-groomed turf with neatness, cleanliness and beauty. But that lush three inches of green obscures a darker reality. The world uses billions of gallons of gasoline each year to shear lawns with mowers that cough astounding quantities of carbon dioxide and other pollutants into the air. In most places, lawns guzzle half of the drinking water available, though much of this runs off the compacted soil rather than soaking into it, carrying pesticides and fertilizers into storm sewers and nearby watercourses. And these lawns are so obsessively homogenized that they can support little more life than the humans walking, lounging and playing on top of it. So here's a better plan: Replace the green monotony in your yard with plantings well suited to the light and climate, and varied in texture and color—less genteel, perhaps, but certainly more interesting.

Photograph: Franco Fontana

Last Night

What did artist and designer *Luke Edward Hall* do with his evening?

GOOD IDEA

by Pip Usher

Forget the prim hedgerows and labor-intensive pruning of a manicured lawn. These days, green-thumbed enthusiasts are embracing wildflower meadows, which require less effort and provide welcoming habitats for pollinators including moths and bees. Although separated into two categories—a perennial meadow, which thrives in nutrient-poor soil, and an annual meadow, which requires more fertile ground—each showcases the distinctive flora that grows naturally and easily in its local environment. For those wanting to try it in their own backyards, there are tomes that offer guidance, such as *Meadows: At Great Dixters and Beyond* by master gardener Christopher Lloyd. Alternatively, simply stop mowing and see what sprouts.

With a particular penchant for Greek mythology and Cecil Beaton, Luke Edward Hall is a designer whose work interprets history with color, playfulness and romanticism. Working across illustration, painting, ceramics and interior design, as well as brand collaborations on porcelain and embroidered slippers, the 30-year-old divides his time between London and—particularly this year—a cottage in countryside.

BG: *What did you do last night?* **LEH:** My boyfriend, Duncan, and I made a chicken pie for supper, and played with our new whippet, Merlin, with *Poirot* on in the background. I love Agatha Christie! We'd thought about getting a dog for a long time and now we're in the middle of intense puppy training. Our flat in Camden is a shoebox. Here, there's more space.

BG: *Where are you?* **LEH:** We've rented this house in Gloucestershire since June last year, and although we were spending mostly weekends here, we see it as our "proper" home. Now, we've been here for six weeks. I feel very lucky to be in the countryside. We live in one of maybe 15 cottages on a small private estate. You can't see any other buildings, even though there's an A-road five minutes away. It's very green, we have cows in the nearby fields and there will be tons of pheasants soon. We have a little barn, too.

BG: *How does country life suit you?* **LEH:** We've really got into gardening. Our evening ritual is to stop work at six, and walk around the garden at dusk to look at our flowers, with a Campari and soda—the sunset is amazing here. We've been planting lots of tulips, like a thousand bulbs; it's crazy.

BG: *What are you doing with the long evenings in?* **LEH:** For better or worse I have got majorly into eBay. I just bought a whole set of *World of Interiors* for £80. I've turned the guest bedroom into a little studio, but I have limited materials here; some gouache and watercolors, a big scanner, but not the full range. I'm making the most of what I've got with me, just trying to keep that ship sailing.

Tyler has cited sociologist Erving Goffman's studies of the meaning of gestures in personal interactions as a huge influence on her observational writing.

The author of sprawling family dramas on her own epic half-century of writing.

BEN SHATTUCK

Anne Tyler

At 78, Anne Tyler might have what every writer wants: twenty-two novels to her name, many of which are *New York Times* bestsellers; a devoted and broad readership; nearly unanimous adoration from critics reinforced by the most prestigious literary awards, including a Pulitzer Prize. Tyler, who is known for writing luminously about everyday dramas, was raised in a series of utopian experimental communities in the mountains. "You're really an outsider when you come out of those," she says. Setting most of her novels within families whose dramas feel familiar to many readers, she's made a lifelong career out of explaining our intimate worlds to us.

BS: *You have a famously rigorous process—writing longhand, recording yourself reading aloud, transcribing, rewriting and so on. Have you always worked like that?* **AT:** I wrote the first three novels in, I believe, fairly short periods of time. I had this idea that if you revise it wasn't spontaneous and fresh. Now, it's such a longer process. It's like sinking deeper and deeper in. I always wonder, what would happen if you just kept going forever? You might get to the inner truth of the universe. But the fact is that I've learned to stop—where I stop always is just when I say, "Ugh, I'm gonna throw up if I read this book again."

BS: *What do you think you're giving the reader by revising so much?* **AT:** What I hope I'm giving the reader is the same experience that I'm trying to give myself: what it feels like to be somebody who's not me. By reading aloud, for instance, I'm making sure the dialogue isn't wooden or strange, so that the reader starts feeling that he's really there with whoever the person is, and so he, too, is experiencing another life. What propelled me to write was being curious about other people. I have a lot of memories of being three or four years old, and telling myself stories in bed at night, which used to drive my brother crazy—he would call out in the dark, "Mama, Anne's whispering again!"

BS: *Do you think your upbringing in isolated communities affected how you observe or are interested in people?* **AT:** In those communities, there was a clear feeling of almost being a Martian landing on Earth when we finally moved away from the last one. Years later, when I was in college, some fellow writing student told me he thought that everybody who was a writer needed to have had rheumatic fever first—meaning to be sort of out of the world a little bit and then come in. And I remember thinking, "Oh, maybe growing up in a commune was my rheumatic fever."

BS: *How do you feel about all your success?* **AT:** I love it if I get a literary prize. But I have to say that, in the long run, it's not as meaningful as I might have thought it would be. In other words, that's not the real reward of it. It makes me so happy to be in the middle of a writing day. I start out in the morning dragging my feet—I take my walk, I read the paper, I think, "Oh, do I have to go to my writing room today?" It's a chore. It feels like breaking through the crust of something. But then I get in, look at what I wrote, and say, "Oh, that's not working out." I pick up a pen and change a word, and then I change another word and then all of a sudden it's three hours later. That part makes me so happy.

Photograph: Stephen Voss

The nature of this puzzle lies within its circled letters.

ANNA GUNDLACH

Crossword

ACROSS

1. Geological layer composed of cooled rock
6. Cousin of a gator
10. Husky vehicle
14. Major blood line
15. Red-hot result of some natural explosions
16. Matador's opponent
17. Sticky stuff in the orchestra pit
18. App store patron
19. Of a similar nature
20. Exercise at an archery range
23. "...you know the rest"
24. Facetious "Me??"
25. Is completely at a loss
34. Listed mishaps
35. Like California redwoods
36. Fresh-daisy connection
37. Naturally occurring element found in 1-across
38. To date
39. Incite to action
40. Small kid
41. Neck of the woods
43. Cuisine with gochujang and bibimbap
45. Beyond ancient

48. Lend a hand
49. "Brokeback Mountain" director Lee
50. Relaxing lakeside activity, as seen in this puzzle's theme
58. Start fishing
59. This is what it sounds like when doves cry
60. Suddenly showed excitement
62. Too
63. Asian sea that has almost completely disappeared
64. South American source of natural fiber
65. Bring in crops
66. Into the night
67. Sounds from hounds in pounds

DOWN

1. Mustang or Bronco, but not a lynx or tiger
2. Possible food for a bear
3. Bear seen in constellations
4. Recipe instruction
5. Conversational digression
6. Handheld purse
7. Scratchy voice
8. No longer interested in
9. Snickers layer
10. Kind of intereference rarely seen on modern TVs
11. Mythical prankster
12. ___ Holder, first Black U.S. Attorney General
13. Ready to eat
21. "At Last" singer James
22. Natural heating source
25. Natural formation at a river's mouth
26. "The Most Stuf" cookies
27. Greek muse of poetry
28. Crestfallen
29. Really got to
30. Brewer's vessel
31. Place for a small microphone
32. Orthodox
33. Pulls in

38. "Naturally!"
39. Mumbai Mr.
41. Go for ___ (try out the water)
42. Like, totally bodacious
43. Secret identity of comic fame
44. "Well, jeepers!"
46. Folding screen?
47. A real pain in the neck
50. Sign of healing
51. Nutrient-rich green
52. "Insecure" star Rae
53. Romcom filmmaker Ephron
54. Kind of cheese
55. The world's longest river
56. Plus others, at the end of a list
57. Basement drainage pit
61. Loudspeakers, for short

Correction

On the shaky science behind Stockholm syndrome.

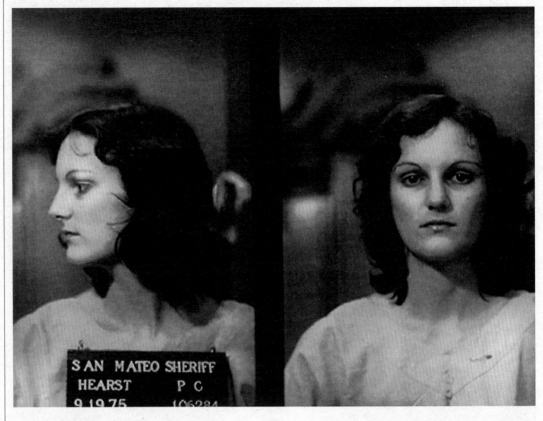

SAN MATEO SHERIFF
HEARST   P C
9 19 75   106284

In 1973, Sweden was gripped by a sensational heist that saw four bank workers taken hostage by a criminal named Jan-Erik Olsson and an accomplice. Over the course of the six-day standoff between Olsson and the police, one of the captives—Kristin Enmark—developed a rapport with the jailers and displayed fear of the Swedish authorities attempting to free her. Following Enmark's release, this reaction was pathologized by the psychiatrist who led the police's efforts, and the term "Stockholm syndrome" was born.

In the years since, Stockholm syndrome has been expanded to describe any psychological condition in which a victim of abuse forms an emotional attachment to their abuser. It has been immortalized in film, from the abducted heroine who falls in love with her captor in *Buffalo '66*, to an adaptation of *3,096 Days*, a memoir written by an Austrian schoolgirl who spent eight years imprisoned in a cellar—and wept when she learned that her tormentor had died. Media outlets and armchair psychologists have been quick to adopt the label—applying it primarily to female victims

In 1974, Patty Hearst—the granddaughter of publishing tycoon William Randolph Hearst—was taken hostage by the Symbionese Liberation Army. After publicly asserting sympathy toward the SLA, she was later seen working with the group to rob banks in San Francisco and was arrested in 1975. Her plea of Stockholm syndrome did not work as a defense in court, although she was later pardoned by President Bill Clinton.

of violence—to explain feelings of dependency and even empathy toward a perpetrator.

A recent book, *See What You Made Me Do*, reveals the insidious sexism that generated the term in the first place. Because Enmark criticized the police's efforts to free her (she felt that their preferred course of action was driven by macho bravado), her anger was dismissed by their psychiatrist as a strange and irrational byproduct of a connection forged with her captors. It was a diagnosis formed without engaging in a conversation with Enmark, let alone undertaking a professional evaluation of her mental state. In short, writes author Jess Hill, it was intended to silence her so that she couldn't embarrass the police.

In the decades since, skepticism of Stockholm syndrome has emerged. The term has not been accepted into either of the leading psychiatric manuals, and professional opinion on its existence remains divided—in fact, it is a diagnosis most often issued in the media. Its suspect backstory serves as a cautionary tale against accepting an idea without first inspecting its origins.

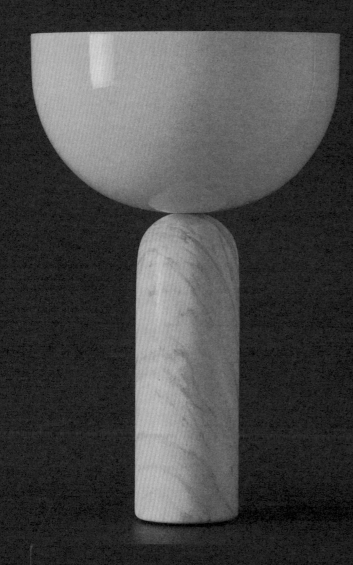

Stockists

ACNE STUDIOS
acnestudios.com

ALIEXPRESS
aliexpress.com

AMI
amiparis.com

ANN DEMEULEMEESTER
anndemeulemeester.com

ANNAKIKI
annakiki.com

ARTHUR AVELLANO
arthuravellano.com

BLUE ERDOS
blueerdos.com

BRUNELLO CUCINELLI
brunocucinelli.com

BURBERRY
burberry.com

BY FAR
byfar.com

CHARVET
charvet.com

DRIES VAN NOTEN
driesvannoten.com

ERIC BOMPARD
ericbompard.com

ERIK JØRGENSEN
erik-joergensen.com

FERRAGAMO
ferragamo.com

GIVENCHY
givenchy.com

GUCCI
gucci.com

HAIDER ACKERMANN
haiderackermann.com

HERMÈS
hermes.com

HOUSE OF FINN JUHL
finnjuhl.com

LAURENCE BOSSION
laurencebossion.com

LOEWE
loewe.com

LOUIS VUITTON
louisvuitton.com

MAISON MARGIELA
maisonmargiela.com

MAISON SANS TITRE
sanstitrestudio.com

MARSET
marset.com

MAX MARA
maxmara.com

MGBW
mgbwhome.com

NANUSHKA
nanushka.com

NINA RICCI
ninaricci.com

PALOMA WOOL
palomawool.com

PARACHUTE HOME
parachutehome.com

PICCOLO SEEDS
piccoloseeds.com

PORTUGUESE FLANNEL
portugueseflannel.com

PRADA
prada.com

SAMSØE & SAMSØE
samsoe.com

STRING
stringfurniture.com

TINA FREY
tinafreydesigns.com

TOMMY ZHONG
tommyzhong.com

UNDERCOVER
undercoverism.com

UNIQLO
uniqlo.com

VALENTINO
valentino.com